KING LEAR

William Shakespeare

D1491044

SPARK PUBLISHING

PROPERTY OF BCC
WALTON COUNTY PUBLIC
LIBRARY SYSTEM

© 2002, 2007 by Spark Publishing

All rights reserved. No part of this publication may be reproduced, stored in a
retrieval system, or transmitted, in any form or by any means, electronic, mechanical,
photocopying, recording, or otherwise, without prior written permission from the
publisher.

SPARKNOTES is a registered trademark of SparkNotes LLC

Spark Publishing
A Division of Barnes & Noble
120 Fifth Avenue
New York, NY 10011
www.sparknotes.com

ISBN-13: 978-1-4114-0720-6
ISBN-10: 1-4114-0720-2

Please submit changes or report errors to www.sparknotes.com/errors.

Printed in the United States

10 9 8 7 6 5 4 3 2 1

CONTENTS

CONTEXT

THE MOST INFLUENTIAL WRITER in all of English literature, William Shakespeare was born in 1564 to a successful middle-class glove-maker in Stratford-upon-Avon, England. Shakespeare attended grammar school, but his formal education proceeded no further. In 1582 he married an older woman, Anne Hathaway, and had three children with her. Around 1590 he left his family behind and traveled to London to work as an actor and playwright. Public and critical success quickly followed, and Shakespeare eventually became the most popular playwright in England and part-owner of the Globe Theater. His career bridged the reigns of Elizabeth I (ruled 1558–1603) and James I (ruled 1603–1625), and he was a favorite of both monarchs. Indeed, James granted Shakespeare's company the greatest possible compliment by bestowing upon its members the title of King's Men. Wealthy and renowned, Shakespeare retired to Stratford and died in 1616 at the age of fifty-two. At the time of Shakespeare's death, literary luminaries such as Ben Jonson hailed his works as timeless.

Shakespeare's works were collected and printed in various editions in the century following his death, and by the early eighteenth century his reputation as the greatest poet ever to write in English was well established. The unprecedented admiration garnered by his works led to a fierce curiosity about Shakespeare's life, but the dearth of biographical information has left many details of Shakespeare's personal history shrouded in mystery. Some people have concluded from this fact and from Shakespeare's modest education that Shakespeare's plays were actually written by someone else— Francis Bacon and the Earl of Oxford are the two most popular candidates—but support for this claim is overwhelmingly circumstantial, and the theory is not taken seriously by many scholars.

In the absence of credible evidence to the contrary, Shakespeare must be viewed as the author of the thirty-seven plays and 154 sonnets that bear his name. The legacy of this body of work is immense. A number of Shakespeare's plays seem to have transcended even the category of brilliance, becoming so influential as to affect profoundly the course of Western literature and culture ever after.

Shakespeare authored *King Lear* around 1605, between *Othello* and *Macbeth*, and it is usually ranked with *Hamlet* as one of Shakespeare's greatest plays. The setting of *King Lear* is as far removed from Shakespeare's time as the setting of any of his other plays, dramatizing events from the eighth century B.C. But the parallel stories of Lear's and Gloucester's sufferings at the hands of their own children reflect anxieties that would have been close to home for Shakespeare's audience. One possible event that may have influenced this play is a lawsuit that occurred not long before *King Lear* was written, in which the eldest of three sisters tried to have her elderly father, Sir Brian Annesley, declared insane so that she could take control of his property. Annesley's youngest daughter, Cordell, successfully defended her father against her sister. Another event that Shakespeare and his audience would have been familiar with is the case of William Allen, a mayor of London who was treated very poorly by his three daughters after dividing his wealth among them. Not least among relevant developments was the then recent transfer of power from Elizabeth I to James I, which occurred in 1603. Elizabeth had produced no male heir, and the anxiety about who her successor would be was fueled by fears that a dynastic struggle along the lines of the fifteenth-century Wars of the Roses might ensue.

Elizabethan England was an extremely hierarchical society, demanding that absolute deference be paid and respect be shown not only to the wealthy and powerful but also to parents and the elderly. *King Lear* demonstrates how vulnerable parents and noblemen are to the depredations of unscrupulous children and thus how fragile the fabric of Elizabethan society actually was.

PLOT OVERVIEW

L EAR, THE AGING KING OF BRITAIN, decides to step down from the throne and divide his kingdom evenly among his three daughters. First, however, he puts his daughters through a test, asking each to tell him how much she loves him. Goneril and Regan, Lear's older daughters, give their father flattering answers. But Cordelia, Lear's youngest and favorite daughter, remains silent, saying that she has no words to describe how much she loves her father. Lear flies into a rage and disowns Cordelia. The king of France, who has courted Cordelia, says that he still wants to marry her even without her land, and she accompanies him to France without her father's blessing.

Lear quickly learns that he made a bad decision. Goneril and Regan swiftly begin to undermine the little authority that Lear still holds. Unable to believe that his beloved daughters are betraying him, Lear slowly goes insane. He flees his daughters' houses to wander on a heath during a great thunderstorm, accompanied by his Fool and by Kent, a loyal nobleman in disguise.

Meanwhile, an elderly nobleman named Gloucester also experiences family problems. His illegitimate son, Edmund, tricks him into believing that his legitimate son, Edgar, is trying to kill him. Fleeing the manhunt that his father has set for him, Edgar disguises himself as a crazy beggar and calls himself "Poor Tom." Like Lear, he heads out onto the heath.

When the loyal Gloucester realizes that Lear's daughters have turned against their father, he decides to help Lear in spite of the danger. Regan and her husband, Cornwall, discover him helping Lear, accuse him of treason, blind him, and turn him out to wander the countryside. He ends up being led by his disguised son, Edgar, toward the city of Dover, where Lear has also been brought.

In Dover, a French army lands as part of an invasion led by Cordelia in an effort to save her father. Edmund apparently becomes romantically entangled with both Regan and Goneril, whose husband, Albany, is increasingly sympathetic to Lear's cause. Goneril and Edmund conspire to kill Albany.

The despairing Gloucester tries to commit suicide, but Edgar saves him by pulling the strange trick of leading him off an imaginary cliff. Meanwhile, the English troops reach Dover, and the

English, led by Edmund, defeat the Cordelia-led French. Lear and Cordelia are captured. In the climactic scene, Edgar duels with and kills Edmund; we learn of the death of Gloucester; Goneril poisons Regan out of jealousy over Edmund and then kills herself when her treachery is revealed to Albany; Edmund's betrayal of Cordelia leads to her needless execution in prison; and Lear finally dies out of grief at Cordelia's passing. Albany, Edgar, and the elderly Kent are left to take care of the country under a cloud of sorrow and regret.

CHARACTER LIST

King Lear The aging king of Britain and the protagonist of the play. Lear is used to enjoying absolute power and to being flattered, and he does not respond well to being contradicted or challenged. At the beginning of the play, his values are notably hollow—he prioritizes the appearance of love over actual devotion and wishes to maintain the power of a king while unburdening himself of the responsibility. Nevertheless, he inspires loyalty in subjects such as Gloucester, Kent, Cordelia, and Edgar, all of whom risk their lives for him.

Cordelia Lear's youngest daughter, disowned by her father for refusing to flatter him. Cordelia is held in extremely high regard by all of the good characters in the play—the king of France marries her for her virtue alone, overlooking her lack of dowry. She remains loyal to Lear despite his cruelty toward her, forgives him, and displays a mild and forbearing temperament even toward her evil sisters, Goneril and Regan. Despite her obvious virtues, Cordelia's reticence makes her motivations difficult to read, as in her refusal to declare her love for her father at the beginning of the play.

Goneril Lear's ruthless oldest daughter and the wife of the duke of Albany. Goneril is jealous, treacherous, and amoral. Shakespeare's audience would have been particularly shocked at Goneril's aggressiveness, a quality that it would not have expected in a female character. She challenges Lear's authority, boldly initiates an affair with Edmund, and wrests military power away from her husband.

Regan Lear's middle daughter and the wife of the duke of Cornwall. Regan is as ruthless as Goneril and as aggressive in all the same ways. In fact, it is difficult to think of any quality that distinguishes her from

5

her sister. When they are not egging each other on to further acts of cruelty, they jealously compete for the same man, Edmund.

Gloucester A nobleman loyal to King Lear whose rank, earl, is below that of duke. The first thing we learn about Gloucester is that he is an adulterer, having fathered a bastard son, Edmund. His fate is in many ways parallel to that of Lear: he misjudges which of his children to trust. He appears weak and ineffectual in the early acts, when he is unable to prevent Lear from being turned out of his own house, but he later demonstrates that he is also capable of great bravery.

Edgar Gloucester's older, legitimate son. Edgar plays many different roles, starting out as a gullible fool easily tricked by his brother, then assuming a disguise as a mad beggar to evade his father's men, then carrying his impersonation further to aid Lear and Gloucester, and finally appearing as an armored champion to avenge his brother's treason. Edgar's propensity for disguises and impersonations makes it difficult to characterize him effectively.

Edmund Gloucester's younger, illegitimate son. Edmund resents his status as a bastard and schemes to usurp Gloucester's title and possessions from Edgar. He is a formidable character, succeeding in almost all of his schemes and wreaking destruction upon virtually all of the other characters.

Kent A nobleman of the same rank as Gloucester who is loyal to King Lear. Kent spends most of the play disguised as a peasant, calling himself "Caius," so that he can continue to serve Lear even after Lear banishes him. He is extremely loyal, but he gets himself into trouble throughout the play by being extremely blunt and outspoken.

Albany   The husband of Lear's daughter Goneril. Albany is good at heart, and he eventually denounces and opposes the cruelty of Goneril, Regan, and Cornwall. Yet he is indecisive and lacks foresight, realizing the evil of his allies quite late in the play.

Cornwall   The husband of Lear's daughter Regan. Unlike Albany, Cornwall is domineering, cruel, and violent, and he works with his wife and sister-in-law Goneril to persecute Lear and Gloucester.

Fool   Lear's jester, who uses double-talk and seemingly frivolous songs to give Lear important advice.

Oswald   The steward, or chief servant, in Goneril's house. Oswald obeys his mistress's commands and helps her in her conspiracies.

CHARACTER LIST

ANALYSIS OF MAJOR CHARACTERS

KING LEAR

Lear's basic flaw at the beginning of the play is that he values appearances above reality. He wants to be treated as a king and to enjoy the title, but he doesn't want to fulfill a king's obligations of governing for the good of his subjects. Similarly, his test of his daughters demonstrates that he values a flattering public display of love over real love. He doesn't ask "which of you doth love us most," but rather, "which of you shall we say doth love us most?" (I.i.49). Most readers conclude that Lear is simply blind to the truth, but Cordelia is already his favorite daughter at the beginning of the play, so presumably he knows that she loves him the most. Nevertheless, Lear values Goneril and Regan's fawning over Cordelia's sincere sense of filial duty.

An important question to ask is whether Lear develops as a character—whether he learns from his mistakes and becomes a better and more insightful human being. In some ways the answer is no: he doesn't completely recover his sanity and emerge as a better king. But his values do change over the course of the play. As he realizes his weakness and insignificance in comparison to the awesome forces of the natural world, he becomes a humble and caring individual. He comes to cherish Cordelia above everything else and to place his own love for Cordelia above every other consideration, to the point that he would rather live in prison with her than rule as a king again.

CORDELIA

Cordelia's chief characteristics are devotion, kindness, beauty, and honesty—honesty to a fault, perhaps. She is contrasted throughout the play with Goneril and Regan, who are neither honest nor loving, and who manipulate their father for their own ends. By refusing to take part in Lear's love test at the beginning of the play, Cordelia establishes herself as a repository of virtue, and the obvious authenticity of her love for Lear makes clear the extent of the king's error in banishing her. For most of the middle section of the play, she is off-stage, but as we observe the depredations of Goneril and Regan and watch Lear's descent into madness, Cordelia is never far from the audience's thoughts, and her beauty is venerably described in religious terms. Indeed, rumors of her return to Britain begin to surface almost immediately, and once she lands at Dover, the action of the play begins to move toward her, as all the characters converge on the coast. Cordelia's reunion with Lear marks the apparent restoration of order in the kingdom and the triumph of love and forgiveness over hatred and spite. This fleeting moment of familial happiness makes the devastating finale of *King Lear* that much more cruel, as Cordelia, the personification of kindness and virtue, becomes a literal sacrifice to the heartlessness of an apparently unjust world.

EDMUND

Of all of the play's villains, Edmund is the most complex and sympathetic. He is a consummate schemer, a Machiavellian character eager to seize any opportunity and willing to do anything to achieve his goals. However, his ambition is interesting insofar as it reflects not only a thirst for land and power but also a desire for the recognition denied to him by his status as a bastard. His serial treachery is not merely self-interested; it is a conscious rebellion against the social order that has denied him the same status as Gloucester's legitimate son, Edgar. "Now, gods, stand up for bastards," Edmund commands, but in fact he depends not on divine aid but on his own initiative (I.ii.22). He is the ultimate self-made man, and he is such a cold and capable villain that it is entertaining to watch him work, much as the audience can appreciate the clever wickedness of Iago in *Othello*. Only at the close of the play does Edmund show a flicker of weakness. Mortally wounded, he sees that both Goneril and Regan have died for him, and whispers, "Yet Edmund was beloved" (V.iii.238). After this ambiguous statement, he seems to repent of his villainy and admits to having ordered Cordelia's death. His peculiar change of heart, rare among Shakespearean villains, is enough to make the audience wonder, amid the carnage, whether Edmund's villainy sprang not from some innate cruelty but simply from a thwarted, misdirected desire for the familial love that he witnessed around him.

GONERIL AND REGAN

There is little good to be said for Lear's older daughters, who are largely indistinguishable in their villainy and spite. Goneril and Regan are clever—or at least clever enough to flatter their father in the play's opening scene—and, early in the play, their bad behavior toward Lear seems matched by his own pride and temper. But any sympathy that the audience can muster for them evaporates quickly, first when they turn their father out into the storm at the end of Act II and then when they viciously put out Gloucester's eyes in Act III. Goneril and Regan are, in a sense, personifications of evil—they have no conscience, only appetite. It is this greedy ambition that enables them to crush all opposition and make themselves mistresses of Britain. Ultimately, however, this same appetite brings about their undoing. Their desire for power is satisfied, but both harbor sexual desire for Edmund, which destroys their alliance and eventually leads them to destroy each other. Evil, the play suggests, inevitably turns in on itself.

CHARACTER ANALYSIS

THEMES, MOTIFS & SYMBOLS

THEMES

Themes are the fundamental and often universal ideas explored in a literary work.

JUSTICE

King Lear is a brutal play, filled with human cruelty and awful, seemingly meaningless disasters. The play's succession of terrible events raises an obvious question for the characters—namely, whether there is any possibility of justice in the world, or whether the world is fundamentally indifferent or even hostile to humankind. Various characters offer their opinions: "As flies to wanton boys are we to the gods; / They kill us for their sport," Gloucester muses, realizing it foolish for humankind to assume that the natural world works in parallel with socially or morally convenient notions of justice (IV. i.37–38). Edgar, on the other hand, insists that "the gods are just," believing that individuals get what they deserve (V.iii.169). But, in the end, we are left with only a terrifying uncertainty—although the wicked die, the good die along with them, culminating in the awful image of Lear cradling Cordelia's body in his arms. There is goodness in the world of the play, but there is also madness and death, and it is difficult to tell which triumphs in the end.

AUTHORITY VERSUS CHAOS

King Lear is about political authority as much as it is about family dynamics. Lear is not only a father but also a king, and when he gives away his authority to the unworthy and evil Goneril and Regan, he delivers not only himself and his family but all of Britain into chaos and cruelty. As the two wicked sisters indulge their appetite for power and Edmund begins his own ascension, the kingdom descends into civil strife, and we realize that Lear has destroyed not only his own authority but *all* authority in Britain. The stable, hierarchal order that Lear initially represents falls apart and disorder engulfs the realm.

The failure of authority in the face of chaos recurs in Lear's wanderings on the heath during the storm. Witnessing the powerful forces of the natural world, Lear comes to understand that he, like the rest of humankind, is insignificant in the world. This realization proves much more important than the realization of his loss of political control, as it compels him to re-prioritize his values and become humble and caring. With this newfound understanding of himself, Lear hopes to be able to confront the chaos in the political realm as well.

RECONCILIATION

Darkness and unhappiness pervade *King Lear*, and the devastating Act V represents one of the most tragic endings in all of literature. Nevertheless, the play presents the central relationship—that between Lear and Cordelia—as a dramatic embodiment of true, self-sacrificing love. Rather than despising Lear for banishing her, Cordelia remains devoted, even from afar, and eventually brings an army from a foreign country to rescue him from his tormentors. Lear, meanwhile, learns a tremendously cruel lesson in humility and eventually reaches the point where he can reunite joyfully with Cordelia and experience the balm of her forgiving love. Lear's recognition of the error of his ways is an ingredient vital to reconciliation with Cordelia, not because Cordelia feels wronged by him but because he has understood the sincerity and depth of her love for him. His maturation enables him to bring Cordelia back into his good graces, a testament to love's ability to flourish, even if only fleetingly, amid the horror and chaos that engulf the rest of the play.

MOTIFS

Motifs are recurring structures, contrasts, and literary devices that can help to develop and inform the text's major themes.

MADNESS

Insanity occupies a central place in the play and is associated with both disorder and hidden wisdom. The Fool, who offers Lear insight in the early sections of the play, offers his counsel in a seemingly mad babble. Later, when Lear himself goes mad, the turmoil in his mind mirrors the chaos that has descended upon his kingdom. At the same time, however, it also provides him with important wisdom by reducing him to his bare humanity, stripped of all royal pretensions. Lear thus learns humility. He is joined in his real madness by Edgar's feigned insanity, which also contains nuggets of wisdom for the king to mine. Meanwhile, Edgar's time as a supposedly insane beggar hardens him and prepares him to defeat Edmund at the close of the play.

BETRAYAL

Betrayals play a critical role in the play and show the workings of wickedness in both the familial and political realms—here, brothers betray brothers and children betray fathers. Goneril and Regan's betrayal of Lear raises them to power in Britain, where Edmund, who has betrayed both Edgar and Gloucester, joins them. However, the play suggests that betrayers inevitably turn on one another, showing how Goneril and Regan fall out when they both become attracted to Edmund, and how their jealousies of one another ultimately lead to mutual destruction. Additionally, it is important to remember that the entire play is set in motion by Lear's blind, foolish betrayal of Cordelia's love for him, which reinforces that at the heart of every betrayal lies a skewed set of values.

SYMBOLS

Symbols are objects, characters, figures, and colors used to represent abstract ideas or concepts.

THE STORM

As Lear wanders about a desolate heath in Act III, a terrible storm, strongly but ambiguously symbolic, rages overhead. In part, the storm echoes Lear's inner turmoil and mounting madness: it is a physical, turbulent natural reflection of Lear's internal confusion. At the same time, the storm embodies the awesome power of nature, which forces the powerless king to recognize his own mortality and human frailty and to cultivate a sense of humility for the first time. The storm may also symbolize some kind of divine justice, as if nature itself is angry about the events in the play. Finally, the meteorological chaos also symbolizes the political disarray that has engulfed Lear's Britain.

BLINDNESS

Gloucester's physical blindness symbolizes the metaphorical blindness that grips both Gloucester and the play's other father figure, Lear. The parallels between the two men are clear: both have loyal children and disloyal children, both are blind to the truth, and both end up banishing the loyal children and making the wicked one(s) their heir(s). Only when Gloucester has lost the use of his eyes and Lear has gone mad does each realize his tremendous error. It is appropriate that the play brings them together near Dover in Act IV to commiserate about how their blindness to the truth about their children has cost them dearly.

SYMBOLS

Summary & Analysis

SUMMARY: ACT I, SCENE I

> *Unhappy that I am, I cannot heave*
> *My heart into my mouth.*
>
> *(See* QUOTATIONS, *p. 51)*

The play begins with two noblemen, Gloucester and Kent, discussing the fact that King Lear is about to divide his kingdom. Their conversation quickly changes, however, when Kent asks Gloucester to introduce his son. Gloucester introduces Edmund, explaining that Edmund is a bastard being raised away from home, but that he nevertheless loves his son dearly.

Lear, the ruler of Britain, enters his throne room and announces his plan to divide the kingdom among his three daughters. He intends to give up the responsibilities of government and spend his old age visiting his children. He commands his daughters to say which of them loves him the most, promising to give the greatest share to that daughter.

Lear's scheming older daughters, Goneril and Regan, respond to his test with flattery, telling him in wildly overblown terms that they love him more than anything else. But Cordelia, Lear's youngest (and favorite) daughter, refuses to speak. When pressed, she says that she cannot "heave her heart into her mouth," that she loves him exactly as much as a daughter should love her father, and that her sisters wouldn't have husbands if they loved their father as much as they say (I.i.90–91). In response, Lear flies into a rage, disowns Cordelia, and divides her share of the kingdom between her two sisters.

The earl of Kent, a nobleman who has served Lear faithfully for many years, is the only courtier who disagrees with the king's actions. Kent tells Lear he is insane to reward the flattery of his older daughters and disown Cordelia, who loves him more than her sisters do. Lear turns his anger on Kent, banishing him from the kingdom and telling him that he must be gone within six days.

The king of France and duke of Burgundy are at Lear's court, awaiting his decision as to which of them will marry Cordelia. Lear calls them in and tells them that Cordelia no longer has any title or land. Burgundy withdraws his offer of marriage, but France is impressed by Cordelia's honesty and decides to make her his queen. Lear sends her away without his blessing.

Goneril and Regan scheme together in secrecy. Although they recognize that they now have complete power over the kingdom, they agree that they must act to reduce their father's remaining authority.

SUMMARY: ACT I, SCENE II

> Thou, nature, art my goddess; to thy law
> My services are bound.
>
> . . .
>
> Now, gods, stand up for bastards!
>
> *(See* QUOTATIONS, *p. 52)*

Edmund enters and delivers a soliloquy expressing his dissatisfaction with society's attitude toward bastards. He bitterly resents his legitimate half-brother, Edgar, who stands to inherit their father's estate. He resolves to do away with Edgar and seize the privileges that society has denied him.

Edmund begins his campaign to discredit Edgar by forging a letter in which Edgar appears to plot the death of their father, Gloucester. Edmund makes a show of hiding this letter from his father and so, naturally, Gloucester demands to read it. Edmund answers his father with careful lies, so that Gloucester ends up thinking that his legitimate son, Edgar, has been scheming to kill him in order to hasten his inheritance of Gloucester's wealth and lands. Later, when Edmund talks to Edgar, he tells him that Gloucester is very angry with him and that Edgar should avoid him as much as possible and carry a sword with him at all times. Thus, Edmund carefully arranges circumstances so that Gloucester will be certain that Edgar is trying to murder him.

ANALYSIS: ACT I, SCENES I–II

The love test at the beginning of Act I, scene i, sets the tone for this extremely complicated play, which is full of emotional subtlety, conspiracy, and double-talk, and which swings between confusing extremes of love and anger. Lear's demand that his daughters express how much they love him is puzzling and hints at the insecurity and fear of an old man who needs to be reassured of his own importance. Of course, rather than being a true assessment of his daughters' love for him, the test seems to invite—or even to demand—flattery. Goneril's and Regan's professions of love are obviously nothing but flattery: Goneril cannot even put her alleged love into words: "A love that makes . . . speech unable / Beyond all manner of so much I love you" (I.i.59); Regan follows her sister's lead by saying, "I find she names my very deed of love; Only she comes too short" (I.i.70–71).

In contrast to her sisters, whose professions are banal and insincere, Cordelia does not seem to know how to flatter her father—an immediate reflection of her honesty and true devotion to him. "Love, and be silent," she says to herself (I.i.60). When her father asks her the crucial question—what she can say to merit the greatest inheritance—she answers only, "Nothing, my lord," and thus seals her fate (I.i.86). Cordelia's authentic love and Lear's blindness to its existence trigger the tragic events that follow.

The shift of the play's focus to Gloucester and Edmund in Act I, scene ii, suggests parallels between this subplot and Lear's familial difficulties. Both Lear and Gloucester have children who are truly loyal to them (Cordelia and Edgar, respectively) and children who are planning to do them harm (Goneril and Regan, and Edmund, respectively); both fathers mistake the unloving for the loving, banishing the loyal children and designating the wicked ones their heirs. This symbolic blindness to the truth becomes more literal as the play progresses—in Lear's eventual madness and Gloucester's physical blinding.

Moreover, Gloucester's willingness to believe the lies that Edmund tells him about Edgar seems to reflect a preexisting fear: that his children secretly want to destroy him and take his power. Ironically, this is what *Edmund*, of course, wants to do to Gloucester, but Gloucester is blind to Edmund's treachery. Gloucester's inability to see the truth echoes the discussion between Goneril and Regan at the end of Act I, scene i, about Lear's unreliability in his old age: the "infirmity of his age" (I.i.291) and his "unconstant starts" (I.i.298) evoke images of senility and suggest that his daughters ought to take control from him, just as Edmund is taking control from Gloucester.

Edmund is significantly more complicated than the other major villains in the play, Regan and Goneril. He schemes against his father's life, but not just because he wants to inherit his wealth and land; indeed, his principal motive seems to be desire for *recognition* and perhaps even the love denied him because of his bastard status. The first time we see Edmund, at the beginning of Act I, scene i, his own father is mocking him because he is illegitimate. Edmund's treachery can be seen as a rebellion against the social hierarchy that makes him worthless in the eyes of the world. He rejects the "plague of custom" (I.ii.3) that makes society disdain him and dedicates himself to "nature" (I.ii.1)—that is, raw, unconstrained existence. He will not be the only character to invoke nature in the course of the play—the complicated relationships that obtain among the natural world, the gods above, and fate or justice pervade the entire play.

Act I, scenes iii–v

Summary: Act I, scene iii

Lear is spending the first portion of his retirement at Goneril's castle. Goneril complains to her steward, Oswald, that Lear's knights are becoming "riotous" and that Lear himself is an obnoxious guest (I.iii.6). Seeking to provoke a confrontation, she orders her servants to behave rudely toward Lear and his attendants.

Summary: Act I, scene iv

Disguised as a simple peasant, Kent appears in Goneril's castle, calling himself Caius. He puts himself in Lear's way, and after an exchange of words in which Caius emphasizes his plainspokenness and honesty, Lear accepts him into service.

Lear's servants and knights notice that Goneril's servants no longer obey their commands. When Lear asks Oswald where Goneril is, Oswald rudely leaves the room without replying. Oswald soon returns, but his disrespectful replies to Lear's questions induce Lear to strike him. Kent steps in to aid Lear and trips Oswald.

The Fool arrives and, in a series of puns and double entendres, tells Lear that he has made a great mistake in handing over his power to Goneril and Regan. After a long delay, Goneril herself arrives to speak with Lear. She tells him that his servants and knights have been so disorderly that he will have to send some of them away whether he likes it or not.

Lear is shocked at Goneril's treasonous betrayal. Nonetheless, Goneril remains adamant in her demand that Lear send away half of his one hundred knights. An enraged Lear repents ever handing his power over to Goneril. He curses his daughter, calling on Nature to make her childless. Surprised by his own tears, he calls for his horses. He declares that he will stay with Regan, whom he believes will be a true daughter and give him the respect that he deserves. When Lear has gone, Goneril argues with her husband, Albany, who is upset with the harsh way she has treated Lear. She says that she has written a letter to her sister Regan, who is likewise determined not to house Lear's hundred knights.

SUMMARY: ACT I, SCENE V
Lear sends Kent to deliver a message to Gloucester. The Fool needles Lear further about his bad decisions, foreseeing that Regan will treat Lear no better than Goneril did. Lear calls on heaven to keep him from going mad. Lear and his attendants leave for Regan's castle.

ANALYSIS: ACT I, SCENES III–V
In these scenes, the tragedy of the play begins to unfold. It is now becoming clear to everyone that Lear has made a mistake in handing over his power to Goneril and Regan. Lear's major error is that, in stepping down from the throne, he has also given up all of his formal authority to those who do not actually love him. He no longer has the power to command anyone to do anything, even to give him shelter or food—his daughters, each of whom is now a queen over half of Britain, wield special authority over him.

Goneril and, as we soon discover, Regan enjoy being in power and conspire to destroy Lear's remaining influence. Their plan to whittle down Lear's retinue from a hundred knights to fifty may not seem devious, but they will soon purge his knights altogether. This gradual diminishment of Lear's attendants symbolizes the gradual elimination of his remaining power. Knights and servants are part of the pomp that surrounds a powerful king, and Lear rightly sees his loss of them as representative of his daughter's declining respect for his rank.

Goneril, of course, says that the reason she demands this reduction is that the knights have been loud and destructive in her castle—they are, she claims, "men so disordered, so deboshed and bold" (I.iv.217). To be fair, it is difficult for us, as readers, to know how true this assertion is. Lear claims, "My train are men of choice and rarest parts, / That all particulars of duty know," yet we have already seen Lear make imperious demands and lose his temper in a seemingly unjustified way (I.iv.240–241). At this point in the play, the audience may still be unsure about whether or not to sympathize with Lear, especially given his capricious decision to banish

Cordelia. Still, we know that Goneril has been talking, in private, about how best to control her aging father.

Lear seems to begin to question his own identity. When he realizes that Goneril plans to frustrate his desires, he asks, "Doth any here know me? This is not Lear. / . . . / Who is it that can tell me who I am?" (I.iv.201–205). It is as if Goneril's insistence that Lear is now senile makes Lear himself wonder whether he is really himself anymore or whether he has lost his mind. Driven to despair at the end of Act I, scene v, he says, "O let me not be mad, not mad, sweet heaven!"—a foreshadowing of his eventual insanity (I.v.38).

In Act I, scene iv, we meet Lear's Fool. Many of Shakespeare's plays feature a clown of some sort, and *King Lear* arguably has two such clowns: the Fool himself and Edgar in his later disguise as Tom O'Bedlam. Many kings and queens during the Renaissance had court fools to amuse them. However, in addition to wearing funny costumes, singing, performing acrobatic tricks, and juggling, fools also made puns and rude jokes and offered their take on matters to their sovereigns.

Lear's Fool cleverly combines this sort of foolishness with a deeper wisdom. The license, traditionally granted to official "fools," to say things to their superiors that anybody else would be punished for enables him to counsel Lear, even though he seems only to prattle nonsensically. Moreover, Lear seems to have a very close relationship with his Fool: the Fool calls Lear "nuncle" and Lear calls the Fool "boy." He is always speaking in riddles and songs, but in these scenes his meaning can be understood: he advises Lear to be wary of his daughters. In telling Lear, "I / am better than thou art now; I am a fool, thou art nothing," he hints at the dangerous situation in which Lear has put himself (I.iv.168–169). His ostensibly silly singing—"The hedge-sparrow fed the cuckoo so long / That it had it head bit off by it young"—clearly warns the king that his daughters, each like a traitorous "cuckoo," plan to turn against the father who raised them (I.iv.190–191).

SUMMARY & ANALYSIS

ACT II, SCENES I–II

Note: Many editions of KING LEAR, *including* THE NORTON SHAKESPEARE, *divide Act II into four scenes. Other editions divide Act II into only two scenes.*

SUMMARY: ACT II, SCENE I

In Gloucester's castle, Gloucester's servant Curan tells Edmund that he has informed Gloucester that the duke of Cornwall and his wife, Regan, are coming to the castle that very night. Curan also mentions vague rumors about trouble brewing between the duke of Cornwall and the duke of Albany.

Edmund is delighted to hear of Cornwall's visit, realizing that he can make use of him in his scheme to get rid of Edgar. Edmund calls Edgar out of his hiding place and tells him that Cornwall is angry with him for being on Albany's side of their disagreement. Edgar has no idea what Edmund is talking about. Edmund tells Edgar further that Gloucester has discovered his hiding place and that he ought to flee the house immediately under cover of night. When he hears Gloucester coming, Edmund draws his sword and pretends to fight with Edgar, while Edgar runs away. Edmund cuts his arm with his sword and lies to Gloucester, telling him that Edgar wanted him to join in a plot against Gloucester's life and that Edgar tried to kill him for refusing. The unhappy Gloucester praises Edmund and vows to pursue Edgar, sending men out to search for him.

Cornwall and Regan arrive at Gloucester's house. They believe Edmund's lies about Edgar, and Regan asks if Edgar is one of the disorderly knights that attend Lear. Edmund replies that he is, and Regan speculates further that these knights put Edgar up to the idea of killing Gloucester in order to acquire Gloucester's wealth. Regan then asks Gloucester for his advice in answering letters from Lear and Goneril.

SUMMARY: ACT II, SCENE II

Outside Gloucester's castle, Kent, still in peasant disguise, meets Oswald, the chief steward of Goneril's household. Oswald doesn't recognize Kent from their scuffle in Act I, scene iv. Kent roundly abuses Oswald, describing him as cowardly, vain, boastful, over-dressed, servile, and groveling. Oswald still maintains that he doesn't know Kent; Kent draws his sword and attacks him.

Oswald's cries for help bring Cornwall, Regan, and Gloucester. Kent replies rudely to their calls for explanation, and

Cornwall orders him to be punished in the stocks, a wooden device that shackles a person's ankles and renders him immobile. Gloucester objects that this humiliating punishment of Lear's messenger will be seen as disrespectful of Lear himself and that the former king will take offense. But Cornwall and Regan maintain that Kent deserves this treatment for assaulting Goneril's servant, and they put him in the stocks.

After everyone leaves, Kent reads a letter that he has received from Cordelia in which she promises that she will find some way, from her current position in France, to help improve conditions in Britain. The unhappy and resigned Kent dozes off in the stocks.

ANALYSIS: ACT II, SCENES I–II

Edmund's clever scheming to get rid of Edgar shows his cunning and his immorality. His ability to manipulate people calls to mind arguably the greatest of Shakespeare's villains, Iago, from *Othello,* who demonstrates a similar capacity for twisting others to serve his own ends. There is a great deal of irony in Edmund's description to his father of the ways in which Edgar has allegedly schemed against Gloucester's life. Edmund goes so far as to state that Edgar told him that no one would ever believe Edmund's word against his because of Edmund's illegitimate birth. With this remark, Edmund not only calls attention to his bastard status—which is clearly central to his resentful, ambitious approach to life—but proves crafty enough to use it to his advantage.

Gloucester's rejection of Edgar parallels Lear's rejection of Cordelia in Act I, scene i, and reminds us of the similarities between the two unhappy families: Edgar and Cordelia are good children of fathers who reject them in favor of children who do not love them. When Gloucester says, "I never got him"—that is, he never begot, or fathered, him—he seems to be denying that he is actually Edgar's father, just as Lear has disowned Cordelia (II.i.79). On the other hand, when he praises Edmund as a "loyal and natural boy," he seems to be acknowledging him as a true son (II.i.85).

It is somewhat difficult to know what to make of Kent's attack on Oswald. Oswald's eagerness to serve the treacherous Goneril in Act I, scene iv, has established him as one of the play's minor villains, but Kent's barrage of insults and subsequent physical attack on Oswald are clearly unprovoked. Oswald's failure to fight back may be interpreted as cowardice, but one can also interpret it as Oswald does: he says that he chooses not to attack Kent because of Kent's "gray

SUMMARY & ANALYSIS

beard"—at nearly fifty, Kent is an old man and thus no longer suited for fighting (II.ii.55). Kent's attack seems to be rooted in his anger at Goneril's treatment of Lear—"anger hath a privilege" is the excuse that he gives Cornwall and Regan—and his rage at the hypocrisy surrounding Lear's betrayal by his daughters (II.ii.62).

Cornwall's and Regan's decision to put Kent in the stocks reinforces what we have already seen of their disrespect for their father. The stocks were a punishment used on common criminals, and their use on Lear's serving man could easily be interpreted as highly disrespectful to Lear's royal status. Gloucester announces as much when he protests, "Your purposed low correction / Is such as basest and contemned'st wretches / . . . / Are punished with" (II.ii.134–137). Regan, however, ignores his pleas; she almost seems to welcome the idea of inviting Lear's anger.

ACT II, SCENES III–IV

SUMMARY: ACT II, SCENE III
As Kent sleeps in the stocks, Edgar enters. He has thus far escaped the manhunt for him, but he is afraid that he will soon be caught. Stripping off his fine clothing and covering himself with dirt, he turns himself into "poor Tom" (II.iii.20). He states that he will pretend to be one of the beggars who, having been released from insane asylums, wander the countryside constantly seeking food and shelter.

SUMMARY: ACT II, SCENE IV
Lear, accompanied by the Fool and a knight, arrives at Gloucester's castle. Lear spies Kent in the stocks and is shocked that anyone would treat one of his servants so badly. When Kent tells him that Regan and Cornwall put him there, Lear cannot believe it and demands to speak with them. Regan and Cornwall refuse to speak with Lear, however, excusing themselves on the grounds that they are sick and weary from traveling. Lear insists. He has difficulty controlling his emotions, but he finally acknowledges to himself that sickness can make people behave strangely. When Regan and Cornwall eventually appear, Lear starts to tell Regan about Goneril's "sharp-toothed unkindness" toward him (II.iv.128). Regan suggests that Goneril may have been justified in her actions, that Lear is growing old and unreasonable, and that he should return to Goneril and beg her forgiveness.

Lear asks Regan to shelter him, but she refuses. He complains more strenuously about Goneril and falls to cursing her. Much to Lear's dismay, Goneril herself arrives at Gloucester's castle. Regan, who had known from Goneril's letters that she was coming, takes her sister's hand and allies herself with Goneril against their father. They both tell Lear that he is getting old and weak and that he must give up half of his men if he wants to stay with either of his daughters.

Lear, confused, says that he and his hundred men will stay with Regan. Regan, however, responds that she will allow him only twenty-five men. Lear turns back to Goneril, saying that he will be willing to come down to fifty men if he can stay with her. But Goneril is no longer willing to allow him even that many. A moment later, things get even worse for Lear: both Goneril and Regan refuse to allow him any servants.

Outraged, Lear curses his daughters and heads outside, where a wild storm is brewing. Gloucester begs Goneril and Regan to bring Lear back inside, but the daughters prove unyielding and state that it is best to let him do as he will. They order that the doors be shut and locked, leaving their father outside in the threatening storm.

ANALYSIS: ACT II, SCENES III–IV

In these scenes, Shakespeare further develops the psychological focus of the play, which centers on cruelty, betrayal, and madness. Lear watches his daughters betray him, and his inability to believe what he is seeing begins to push him toward the edge of insanity. This movement begins with Lear's disbelief when he sees how Regan has treated his servant Kent. By putting Kent in the stocks, Regan indicates her lack of respect for Lear as king and father. When Lear realizes how badly Regan is treating him, he reacts with what seems to be a dramatically physical upwelling of grief: he cries out, "O, how this mother swells up toward my heart! / *Hysterica passio,* down, thou climbing sorrow" (II.iv.54–55). "The mother" was a Renaissance term for an illness that felt like suffocation; characterized by light-headedness and strong pain in the stomach, its symptoms resemble those of emotional trauma, grief, and hysteria.

Regan clearly tries to undercut Lear's rapidly waning authority. As her subversion becomes clearer, Lear denies it in ways that become more and more painful to watch. Regan and Cornwall refuse his demands to speak with them, and Lear forgets that, since he has given up his power, he can no longer give them orders. Goneril and Regan eventually insult Lear by telling him that he is senile: "I pray you, father, being weak, seem so" (II.iv.196). These barbed words from Regan skirt the issue of Lear's loss of authority and point to something that he can neither deny nor control—that he is growing old.

The sisters' refusal to allow Lear to keep his hundred knights and Regan's polite but steadfast refusal to allow him to stay with her instead of Goneril finally begin to make Lear understand that he can no longer command like a king. But he stands in fierce denial of this loss of authority; being forced to this realization causes him to alternate between grief and an anger so powerful that it seems to be driving him mad. We see flashes of this anger and madness when he curses Goneril, and then, later, when he declares that instead of returning to Goneril's house without servants, he will flee houses entirely and live in the open air.

The servants that Lear wants to keep with him are symbols of more than just his authority. When Regan asks why he needs even one attendant, Lear bursts out, "O, reason not the need!" (II.iv.259). Human nature, he says, would be no different from that of animals if humans never needed more than the fundamental necessities of life. Clearly, Lear needs his servants not because of the service that they provide him but because of what they represent: his authority and his importance—in essence, the identity that he has built for himself. Regan and Goneril, in denying Lear his servants, deny their father that which he needs the most: not what he needs to be a king, but what he needs to be a human being.

Lear's cry of "O fool, I shall go mad!" foreshadows the fate that soon befalls him (II.iv.281). His words also recall the earlier scene in which Edgar dons a disguise and assumes the identity of a "Bedlam beggar" (II.iii.14). "Bedlam" was a nickname for the Bethlehem hospital in Elizabethan London where the mentally ill were housed. When Edgar rips his clothes to shreds and smears himself with dirt, he is taking on the disguise of a "poor Tom" (II.iii.20), one of the insane Bedlam beggars who roam the countryside sticking themselves with pins and begging "with roaring voices" (II.iii.14). Thus, in these scenes, both Lear and Edgar flee from civilization, leaving the safety of walls and roofs behind in favor of the chaos and confusion of the natural world.

Act III, scenes i–iii

Summary: Act III, scene i

A storm rages on the heath. Kent, seeking Lear in vain, runs into one of Lear's knights and learns that Lear is somewhere in the area, accompanied only by his Fool. Kent gives the knight secret information: he has heard that there is unrest between Albany and Cornwall and that there are spies for the French in the English courts. Kent tells the knight to go to Dover, the city in England nearest to France, where he may find friends who will help Lear's cause. He gives the knight a ring and orders him to give it to Cordelia, who will know who has sent the knight when she sees the ring. Kent leaves to search for Lear.

Summary: Act III, scene ii

Meanwhile, Lear wanders around in the storm, cursing the weather and challenging it to do its worst against him. He seems slightly irrational, his thoughts wandering from idea to idea but always returning to fixate on his two cruel daughters. The Fool, who accompanies him, urges him to humble himself before his daughters and seek shelter indoors, but Lear ignores him. Kent finds the two of them and urges them to take shelter inside a nearby hovel. Lear finally agrees and follows Kent toward the hovel. The Fool makes a strange and confusing prophecy.

Summary: Act III, scene iii

Inside his castle, a worried Gloucester speaks with Edmund. The loyal Gloucester recounts how he became uncomfortable when Regan, Goneril, and Cornwall shut Lear out in the storm. But when he urged them to give him permission to go out and help Lear, they became angry, took possession of his castle, and ordered him never to speak to Lear or plead on his behalf.

Gloucester tells Edmund that he has received news of a conflict between Albany and Cornwall. He also informs him that a French army is invading and that part of it has already landed in England. Gloucester feels that he must take Lear's side and now plans to go seek him out in the storm. He tells Edmund that there is a letter with news of the French army locked in his room, and he asks his son to go and distract the duke of Cornwall while he, Gloucester, goes onto the heath to search for Lear. He adds that it is imperative that Cornwall not notice his absence; otherwise, Gloucester might die for his treachery.

When Gloucester leaves, Edmund privately rejoices at the opportunity that has presented itself. He plans to betray his father immediately, going to Cornwall to tell him about both Gloucester's plans to help Lear and the location of the traitorous letter from the French. Edmund expects to inherit his father's title, land, and fortune as soon as Gloucester is put to death.

ANALYSIS: ACT III, SCENES I–III

The information that Kent gives the knight brings the audience out of the personal realm of Lear's anguish and into the political world of Lear's Britain. Throughout the play, we hear rumors of conflict between Albany and Cornwall and of possible war with France, but what exactly transpires at any specific moment is rarely clear. The question of the French is not definitively resolved until Act IV. Kent's mention of Dover, however, provides a clue: Dover is a port city in the south of England where ships from France often landed; it is famous for its high white cliffs. As various characters begin moving southward toward Dover in the scenes that follow, the tension of an inevitable conflict heightens. Whatever the particulars of the political struggle, however, it is clear that Lear, by giving away his power in Britain to Goneril and Regan—and eventually Edmund—has destroyed not only his own authority but *all* authority. Instead of a stable, hierarchical kingdom with Lear in control, chaos has overtaken the realm, and the country is at the mercy of the play's villains, who care for nothing but their own power.

This political chaos is mirrored in the natural world. We find Lear and his courtiers plodding across a deserted heath with winds howling around them and rain drenching them. Lear, like the other characters, is unused to such harsh conditions, and he soon finds himself symbolically stripped bare. He has already discovered that his cruel daughters can victimize him; now he learns that a king caught in a storm is as much subject to the power of nature as any man.

The importance of the storm, and its symbolic connection to the state of mind of the people caught in it, is first suggested by the knight's words to Kent. Kent asks the knight, "Who's there, besides foul weather?"; the knight answers, "One minded like the weather, most unquietly"(III.i.1–2). Here the knight's state of mind is shown to be as turbulent as the winds and clouds surrounding him. This is true of Lear as well: when Kent asks the knight where the king is, the knight replies, "Contending with the fretful elements; / . . . / Strives in his little world of man to out-scorn / The to-and-fro-conflicting wind and rain" (III.i.4–11). Shakespeare's use of pathetic fallacy—a literary device in which inanimate objects such as nature assume human reactions—amplifies the tension of the characters' struggles by elevating human forces to the level of natural forces.

Lear is trying to face down the powers of nature, an attempt that seems to indicate both his despair and his increasingly confused sense of reality. Both of these strains appear in Lear's famous speech to the storm, in which he commands, "Blow, winds, and crack your cheeks! rage! blow! / You cataracts and hurricanoes, spout / Till you have drenched our steeples, drowned the cocks!" (III.ii.1–3). Lear's attempt to speak to the storm suggests that he has lost touch with the natural world and his relation to it—or, at least, that he has lost touch with the ordinary human understanding of nature. In a sense, though, his diatribe against the weather embodies one of the central questions posed by *King Lear*: namely, whether the universe is fundamentally friendly or hostile to man. Lear asks whether nature and the gods are actually good, and, if so, how life can have treated him so badly.

The storm marks one of the first appearances of the apocalyptic imagery that is so important in *King Lear* and that will become increasingly dominant as the play progresses. The chaos reflects the disorder in Lear's increasingly crazed mind, and the apocalyptic language represents the projection of Lear's rage and despair onto the outside world: if his world has come to a symbolic end because his daughters have stripped away his power and betrayed him, then, he seems to think, the real world ought to end, too. As we have seen, the chaos in nature also reflects the very real political chaos that has engulfed Britain in the absence of Lear's authority.

Along with Lear's increasing despair and projection, we also see his understandable fixation on his daughters: "Nor rain, wind, thunder, fire, are my daughters: / I tax you not, you elements, with unkindness" (III.ii.14–15). Lear tells the thunder that he does not blame it for attacking him because it does not owe him anything. But he does blame his "two pernicious daughters" for their betrayal (III.ii.21). Despite the apparent onset of insanity, Lear exhibits some degree of rational thought—he is still able to locate the source of his misfortune.

Finally, we see strange shifts beginning to occur inside Lear's mind. He starts to realize that he is going mad, a terrifying realization for anyone. Nevertheless, Lear suddenly notices his Fool and asks him, "How dost my boy? Art cold?" (III.ii.66). He adds, "I

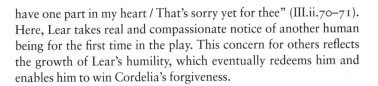

have one part in my heart / That's sorry yet for thee" (III.ii.70–71). Here, Lear takes real and compassionate notice of another human being for the first time in the play. This concern for others reflects the growth of Lear's humility, which eventually redeems him and enables him to win Cordelia's forgiveness.

ACT III, SCENES IV–V

SUMMARY: ACT III, SCENE IV

Kent leads Lear through the storm to the hovel. He tries to get him to go inside, but Lear resists, saying that his own mental anguish makes him hardly feel the storm. He sends his Fool inside to take shelter and then kneels and prays. He reflects that, as king, he took too little care of the wretched and homeless, who have scant protection from storms such as this one.

The Fool runs out of the hovel, claiming that there is a spirit inside. The spirit turns out to be Edgar in his disguise as Tom O'Bedlam. Edgar plays the part of the madman by complaining that he is being chased by a devil. He adds that fiends possess and inhabit his body. Lear, whose grip on reality is loosening, sees nothing strange about these statements. He sympathizes with Edgar, asking him whether bad daughters have been the ruin of him as well.

Lear asks the disguised Edgar what he used to be before he went mad and became a beggar. Edgar replies that he was once a wealthy courtier who spent his days having sex with many women and drinking wine. Observing Edgar's nakedness, Lear tears off his own clothes in sympathy.

Gloucester, carrying a torch, comes looking for the king. He is unimpressed by Lear's companions and tries to bring Lear back inside the castle with him, despite the possibility of evoking Regan and Goneril's anger. Kent and Gloucester finally convince Lear to go with Gloucester, but Lear insists on bringing the disguised Edgar, whom he has begun to like, with him.

SUMMARY: ACT III, SCENE V

Inside Gloucester's castle, Cornwall vows revenge against Gloucester, whom Edmund has betrayed by showing Cornwall a letter that proves Gloucester's secret support of a French invasion. Edmund pretends to be horrified at the discovery of his father's "treason," but he is actually delighted, since the powerful Cornwall, now his ally, confers upon him the title of earl of Gloucester (III.v.10). Cornwall sends Edmund to find Gloucester, and Edmund reasons to himself that if he can catch his father in the act of helping Lear, Cornwall's suspicions will be confirmed.

ANALYSIS: ACT III, SCENES IV–V

When Kent asks Lear to enter the hovel at the beginning of Act III, scene iv, Lear's reply demonstrates that part of his mind is still lucid and that the symbolic connection between the storm outside and Lear's own mental disturbance is significant. Lear explains to Kent that although the storm may be very uncomfortable for Kent, Lear himself hardly notices it: "The tempest in my mind / Doth from my senses take all feeling else" (III.iv.13–14). Lear's sensitivity to the storm is blocked out by his mental and emotional anguish and by his obsession with his treacherous daughters. The only thing that he can think of is their "filial ingratitude" (III.iv.15).

Lear also continues to show a deepening sensitivity to other people, a trait missing from his character at the beginning of the play and an interesting side effect of his increasing madness and exposure to human cruelty. After he sends his Fool into the hovel to take shelter, he kneels in prayer—the first time we have seen him do so in the play. He does not pray for himself; instead, he asks the gods to help "poor naked wretches, wheresoe'er you are, / That bide the pelting of this pitiless storm" (III.iv.29–30). Reproaching himself for his heartlessness, Lear urges himself to "expose thyself to feel what wretches feel" (III.iv.35). This self-criticism and newfound sympathy for the plight of others mark the continuing humanization of Lear.

Lear's obsessive contemplation of his own humanity and of his place in relation to nature and to the gods is heightened still further after he meets Edgar, who is clad only in rags. Lear's wandering mind turns to his own fine clothing, and he asks, addressing Edgar's largely uncovered body, "Is man no more than this? Consider him well" (III.iv.95–96). As a king in fact as well as in name, with servants and subjects and seemingly loyal daughters, Lear could be confident of his place in the universe; indeed, the universe seemed to revolve around him. Now, as his humility grows, he becomes conscious of his real relationship to nature. He is frightened to see himself as little more than a "bare, forked animal," stripped of everything that made him secure and powerful (III.iv.99–100).

The destruction of Lear's pride leads him to question the social order that clothes kings in rich garments and beggars in rags. He realizes that each person, underneath his or her clothing, is naked and therefore weak. He sees too that clothing offers no protection against the forces of the elements or of the gods. When he tries to remove his own clothing, his companions restrain him. But Lear's attempt to bare himself is a sign that he has seen the similarities between himself and Edgar: only the flimsy surface of garments marks the difference between a king and a beggar. Each must face the cruelty of an uncaring world.

The many names that Edgar uses for the demons that pester him seem to have been taken by Shakespeare from a single source—Samuel Harsnett's *A Declaration of Egregious Popish Impostors*, which describes demons in wild and outlandish language to ridicule the exorcisms performed by Catholic priests. Edgar uses similarly strange and haunting language to describe his demons. The audience assumes that he is only feigning madness; after all, we have seen him deliberately decide to pose as a crazed beggar in order to escape capture by his brother and father. But Edgar's ravings are so convincing, and the storm-wracked heath such a bizarre environment, that the line between pretending to be mad and actually *being* mad seems to blur.

ACT III, SCENES VI–VII

SUMMARY: ACT III, SCENE VI
Gloucester, Kent, Lear, and the Fool take shelter in a small building (perhaps a shed or farmhouse) on Gloucester's property. Gloucester leaves to find provisions for the king. Lear, whose mind is wandering ever more widely, holds a mock trial of his wicked daughters, with Edgar, Kent, and the Fool presiding. Both Edgar and the Fool speak like madmen, and the trial is an exercise in hallucination and eccentricity.

Gloucester hurries back in to tell Kent that he has overheard a plot to kill Lear. Gloucester begs Kent to quickly transport Lear toward Dover, in the south of England, where allies will be waiting for him. Gloucester, Kent, and the Fool leave. Edgar remains behind for a moment and speaks in his own, undisguised voice about how much less important his own suffering feels now that he has seen Lear's far worse suffering.

SUMMARY: ACT III, SCENE VII
Back in Gloucester's castle, Cornwall gives Goneril the treasonous letter concerning the French army at Dover and tells her to take it and show it to her husband, Albany. He then sends his servants

PROPERTY OF BCC
WALTON COUNTY PUBLIC
LIBRARY SYSTEM

to apprehend Gloucester so that Gloucester can be punished. He orders Edmund to go with Goneril to Albany's palace so that Edmund will not have to witness the violent punishment of his father.

Oswald brings word that Gloucester has helped Lear escape to Dover. Gloucester is found and brought before Regan and Cornwall. They treat him cruelly, tying him up like a thief, insulting him, and pulling his white beard. Cornwall remarks to himself that he cannot put Gloucester to death without holding a formal trial but that he can still punish him brutally and get away with it.

Admitting that he helped Lear escape, Gloucester swears that he will see Lear's wrongs avenged. Cornwall replies, "See 't shalt thou never," and proceeds to dig out one of Gloucester's eyes, throw it on the floor, and step on it (III.vii.68). Gloucester screams, and Regan demands that Cornwall put out the other eye, too.

One of Gloucester's servants suddenly steps in, saying that he cannot stand by and let this outrage happen. Cornwall draws his sword and the two fight. The servant wounds Cornwall, but Regan grabs a sword from another servant and kills the first servant before he can injure Cornwall further. Irate, the wounded Cornwall gouges out Gloucester's remaining eye.

Gloucester calls out for his son Edmund to help him, but Regan triumphantly tells him that it was Edmund who betrayed him to Cornwall in the first place. Gloucester, realizing immediately that Edgar was the son who really loved him, laments his folly and prays to the gods to help Edgar. Regan and Cornwall order that Gloucester be thrown out of the house to "smell / His way to Dover" (III.vii.96–97). Cornwall, realizing that his wound is bleeding heavily, exits with Regan's aid.

Left alone with Gloucester, Cornwall's and Regan's servants express their shock and horror at what has just happened. They decide to treat Gloucester's bleeding face and hand him over to the mad beggar to lead Gloucester where he will.

ANALYSIS: ACT III, SCENES VI–VII

In these scenes, Shakespeare continues to develop Lear's madness. Lear rages on against his daughters and is encouraged by comments that Edgar and the Fool make. We may interpret the Fool's remark "He's mad that trusts in the tameness of a wolf" as referring to Lear's folly in trusting his two wolflike daughters (III.vi.16). Edgar, for his part, speaks like a madman who sees demons everywhere; since Lear has started to hallucinate that he sees his daughters, the two madmen get along well. For instance, when Lear accosts his absent daughters ("Now, you she foxes!"), Edgar scolds them likewise (III.vi.20). Animal imagery will be applied to Goneril and Regan again later in Lear's mock trial of his daughters: "The little dogs and all, / Tray, Blanch, and Sweet-heart, see, they bark at me" (III.vi.57–58). Having reduced his sense of himself to a "bare, forked animal," he now makes his vicious daughters animals as well—but they, of course, seem like predatory, disloyal creatures to him (III.iv.99–100).

Act III, scene vi, is the Fool's last scene, and Edgar continues to take over the Fool's function by answering Lear's mad words and jingles. When Lear declares, "We'll go to supper i' the morning" (III.vi.77), thus echoing the confusion of the natural order in the play, the Fool answers, "And I'll go to bed at noon" (III.vi.78). This line is the last we hear from him in the play. One can argue that since Lear is sliding into madness, he can no longer understand the nonsense of the Fool, who actually is sane, but rather can relate only to Edgar, who pretends to be mad. One can also argue that Lear has internalized the Fool's criticisms of his own errors, and thus he no longer needs to hear them from an outside source. In any case, the Fool, having served Shakespeare's purpose, has become expendable.

Edgar's speech at the end of Act III, scene vi, in which he leaves off babbling and addresses the audience, gives us a needed reminder that, despite appearances, he is *not* actually insane. We are also reminded, yet again, of the similarities between his situation and Lear's. "He childed as I fathered," says Edgar, suggesting that just as Lear's ungrateful daughters put Lear where he is now, so Gloucester, too willing to believe the evil words of Edmund, did the same to Edgar (III.vi.103).

The shocking violence of Act III, scene vii, is one of the bloodiest onstage actions in all of Shakespeare. Typically, especially in Shakespeare's later plays, murders and mutilations take place offstage. Here, however, the violence happens right before our eyes, with Cornwall's snarl "Out, vile jelly!" as a ghastly complement to the action (III.vii.86). (How graphic our view of the violence is depends on how it is staged.) The horror of Gloucester's blinding marks a turning point in the play: cruelty, betrayal, and even madness may be reversible, but blinding is not. It becomes evident at this point that the chaos and cruelty permeating the play have reached a point of no return.

Indeed, it is hard to overestimate the sheer cruelty that Regan and Cornwall perpetrate, in ways both obvious and subtle, against Gloucester. From Cornwall's order to "pinion him like a thief" (III.vii.23) and Regan's exhortation to tie his arms "hard, hard" (III.vii.32)—a disgraceful way to handle a nobleman—to Regan's astonishing rudeness in yanking on Gloucester's white beard after he is tied down, the two seem intent on hurting and humiliating Gloucester. Once again, the social order is inverted: the young are cruel to the old; loyalty to the old king is punished as treachery to the new rulers; Regan and Cornwall, guests within Gloucester's house, thoroughly violate the age-old conventions of respect and politeness. Cornwall does not have the authority to kill or punish Gloucester without a trial, but he decides to ignore that rule because he can: "Our power / Shall do a courtesy to our wrath, which men / May blame, but not control" (III.vii.25–27).

This violence is mitigated slightly by the unexpected display of humanity on the part of Cornwall's servants. Just as Cornwall and Regan violate a range of social norms, so too do the servants, by challenging their masters. One servant gives his life trying to save Gloucester; others help the injured Gloucester and bring him to the disguised Edgar. Even amid the increasing chaos, some human compassion remains.

Act IV, scenes i–ii

Summary: Act IV, scene i

> As flies to wanton boys are we to the gods;
> They kill us for their sport.

(See QUOTATIONS, *p. 54)*

Edgar talks to himself on the heath, reflecting that his situation is not as bad as it could be. He is immediately presented with the horrifying sight of his blinded father. Gloucester is led by an old man who has been a tenant of both Gloucester and Gloucester's father for eighty years. Edgar hears Gloucester tell the old man that if he could only touch his son Edgar again, it would be worth more to him than his lost eyesight. But Edgar chooses to remain disguised as Poor Tom rather than reveal himself to his father. Gloucester asks the old man to bring some clothing to cover Tom, and he asks Tom to lead him to Dover. Edgar agrees. Specifically, Gloucester asks to be led to the top of the highest cliff.

SUMMARY: ACT IV, SCENE II

Goneril and Edmund arrive outside of her palace, and Goneril expresses surprise that Albany did not meet them on the way. Oswald tells her that Albany is displeased with Goneril's and Regan's actions, glad to hear that the French army had landed, and sorry to hear that Goneril is returning home.

Goneril realizes that Albany is no longer her ally and criticizes his cowardice, resolving to assert greater control over her husband's military forces. She directs Edmund to return to Cornwall's house and raise Cornwall's troops for the fight against the French. She informs him that she will likewise take over power from her husband. She promises to send Oswald with messages. She bids Edmund goodbye with a kiss, strongly hinting that she wants to become his mistress.

As Edmund leaves, Albany enters. He harshly criticizes Goneril. He has not yet learned about Gloucester's blinding, but he is outraged at the news that Lear has been driven mad by Goneril and Regan's abuse. Goneril angrily insults Albany, accusing him of being a coward. She tells him that he ought to be preparing to fight against the French invaders. Albany retorts by calling her monstrous and condemns the evil that she has done to Lear.

A messenger arrives and delivers the news that Cornwall has died from the wound that he received while putting out Gloucester's eyes. Albany reacts with horror to the report of Gloucester's blinding and interprets Cornwall's death as divine retribution. Meanwhile, Goneril displays mixed feelings about Cornwall's death: on the one hand, it makes her sister Regan less powerful; on the other hand, it leaves Regan free to pursue Edmund herself. Goneril leaves to answer her sister's letters.

Albany demands to know where Edmund was when his father was being blinded. When he hears that it was Edmund who betrayed Gloucester and that Edmund left the house specifically so that Cornwall could punish Gloucester, Albany resolves to take revenge upon Edmund and help Gloucester.

ANALYSIS: ACT IV, SCENES I–II

In these scenes, the play moves further and further toward hopelessness. We watch characters who think that matters are improving realize that they are only getting worse. Edgar, wandering the plains half naked, friendless, and hunted, thinks the worst has passed, until the world sinks to another level of darkness, when he glimpses his beloved father blinded, crippled, and bleeding from the eye sockets. Gloucester, who seems to have resigned himself to his sightless future, expresses a similar feeling of despair in one of the play's most famous and disturbing lines: "As flies to wanton boys are we to the gods; / They kill us for their sport" (IV.i.37–38). Here we have nihilism in its starkest form: the idea that there is no order, no goodness in the universe, only caprice and cruelty. This theme of despair in the face of an uncaring universe makes *King Lear* one of Shakespeare's darkest plays. For Gloucester, as for Lear on the heath, there is no possibility of redemption or happiness in the world—there is only the "sport" of vicious, inscrutable gods.

It is unclear why Edgar keeps up his disguise as Poor Tom. Whatever Edgar's (or Shakespeare's) reasoning, his secrecy certainly creates dramatic tension and allows Edgar to continue to babble about the "foul fiend[s]" that possess and follow him (IV.i.59). It also makes him unlikely to ask Gloucester his reasons for wanting to go to Dover. Gloucester phrases his request strangely, asking Tom to lead him only to the brim of the cliff, where "from that place / I shall no leading need" (IV.i.77–78). These lines clearly foreshadow Gloucester's later attempt to commit suicide.

Meanwhile, the characters in power, having blinded Gloucester and driven off Lear, are swiftly becoming divided. The motif of betrayal recurs, but this time it is the wicked betraying the wicked. Cornwall has died, and Albany has turned against his wife, Goneril, and her remaining allies, Regan and Edmund. Albany's unexpected discovery of a conscience after witnessing his wife's cruelty raises the theme of redemption for the first time, offering the possibility that even an apparently wicked character can recover his goodness and try to make amends. Significantly, Albany's attacks on his wife echo Lear's own words: "O Goneril! / You are not worth the dust which the rude wind / Blows in your face," Albany tells her after hearing what she has done to her father (IV.ii.30–32). Like Lear, Albany uses animal imagery to describe the faithless daughters. "Tigers, not daughters, what have you performed?" he asks (IV.ii.41). Goneril, for her part, is hardly intimidated by him; she calls him a "moral fool" for criticizing her while France invades (IV.i.59). Goneril equates Albany's moralizing with foolishness, a sign of her evil nature.

When Albany hears that Cornwall is dead, he thanks divine justice in words that run counter to Gloucester's earlier despair. "This shows you are above, / You justicers," he cries, offering a slightly more optimistic—if grim—take on the possibility of divine justice than Gloucester's earlier comment about flies, boys, and death (IV. ii.79–80). His words imply that perhaps it will be possible to restore order after all, perhaps the wicked characters will yet suffer for their sins—or so the audience and characters alike can hope.

ACT IV, SCENES III–V

SUMMARY: ACT IV, SCENE III
Kent, still disguised as an ordinary serving man, speaks with a gentleman in the French camp near Dover. The gentleman tells Kent that the king of France landed with his troops but quickly departed to deal with a problem at home. Kent's letters have been brought to Cordelia, who is now the queen of France and who has been left in charge of the army. Kent questions the gentleman about Cordelia's reaction to the letters, and the gentleman gives a moving account of Cordelia's sorrow upon reading about her father's mistreatment.

Kent tells the gentleman that Lear, who now wavers unpredictably between sanity and madness, has also arrived safely in Dover. Lear, however, refuses to see Cordelia because he is ashamed of the way he treated her. The gentleman informs Kent that the armies of both Albany and the late Cornwall are on the march, presumably to fight against the French troops.

SUMMARY: ACT IV, SCENE IV
Cordelia enters, leading her soldiers. Lear has hidden from her in the cornfields, draping himself in weeds and flowers and singing madly to himself. Cordelia sends one hundred of her soldiers to find Lear and bring him back. She consults with a doctor about Lear's chances for recovering his sanity. The doctor tells her that what Lear most needs is sleep and that there are medicines that can make him sleep. A messenger brings Cordelia the news that the British armies of Cornwall and Albany are marching toward them. Cordelia expected this news, and her army stands ready to fight.

SUMMARY: ACT IV, SCENE V
Back at Gloucester's castle, Oswald tells Regan that Albany's army has set out, although Albany has been dragging his feet about the expedition. It seems that Goneril is a "better soldier" than Albany (IV.v.4). Regan is extremely curious about the letter that Oswald carries from Goneril to Edmund, but Oswald refuses to show it to her. Regan guesses that the letter concerns Goneril's love affair with

Edmund, and she tells Oswald plainly that she wants Edmund for herself. Regan reveals that she has already spoken with Edmund about this possibility; it would be more appropriate for Edmund to get involved with her, now a widow, than with Goneril, with whom such involvement would constitute adultery. She gives Oswald a token or a letter (the text doesn't specify which) to deliver to Edmund, whenever he may find him. Finally, she promises Oswald a reward if he can find and kill Gloucester.

ANALYSIS: ACT IV, SCENES III–V

In these scenes, we see Cordelia for the first time since Lear banished her in Act I, scene i. The words the gentleman uses to describe Cordelia to Kent seem to present her as a combination idealized female beauty and quasi-religious savior figure. The gentleman uses the language of love poetry to describe her beauty—her lips are "ripe," the tears in her eyes are "as pearls from diamonds dropped," and her "smiles and tears" are like the paradoxically coexisting "sunshine and rain" (IV.iii.17–21). But the gentleman also describes Cordelia in language that might be used to speak of a holy angel or the Virgin Mary herself: he says that, as she wiped away her tears, "she shook / The holy water from her heavenly eyes" (IV.iii.28–29). Cordelia's great love for her father, which contrasts sharply with Goneril and Regan's cruelty, elevates her to the level of reverence.

The strength of Cordelia's daughterly love is reinforced in Act IV, scene iv, when Cordelia orders her people to seek out and help her father. We learn that the main reason for the French invasion of England is Cordelia's desire to help Lear: "great France / My mourning and importuned tears hath pitied," she says (IV.iv.26–27). The king of France, her husband, took pity on her grief and allowed the invasion in an effort to help restore Lear to the throne. When Cordelia proclaims that she is motivated not by ambition but by "love, dear love, and our aged father's right," we are reminded of how badly Lear treated her at the beginning of the play (IV.iv.29). Her virtue and devotion is manifest in her willingness to forgive her father for his awful behavior. At one point, she declares, "O dear father, / It is thy business that I go about" (IV.iv.24–25), echoing a biblical passage in which Christ says, "I must go about my father's business" (Luke 2:49). This allusion reinforces Cordelia's piety and purity and consciously links her to Jesus Christ, who, of course, was a martyr to love, just as Cordelia becomes at the play's close.

The other characters in the play discuss Lear's madness in interesting language, and some of the most memorable turns of phrase in the play come from these descriptions. When Cordelia assesses Lear's condition in Act IV, scene iv, she says he is

> As mad as the vexed sea; singing aloud;
> Crowned with rank fumiter and furrow-weeds,
> With hordocks, hemlock, nettles, cuckoo-flowers,
> Darnel, and all the idle weeds that grow. (IV.iv.2–5)

Lear's madness, which is indicated here by both his singing and his self-adornment with flowers, is marked by an embrace of the natural world; rather than perceiving himself as a heroic figure who transcends nature, he understands that he is a small, meaningless component of it. Additionally, this description brings to mind other famous scenes of madness in Shakespeare—most notably, the scenes of Ophelia's flower-bedecked madness in *Hamlet*.

These scenes set up the resolution of the play's tension, which takes place in Act V. While Lear hides from Cordelia out of shame, she seeks him out of love, crystallizing the contrast between her forgiveness and his repentance. Regan and Goneril have begun to become rivals for the affection of Edmund, as their twin ambitions inevitably bring them into conflict. On the political and military level, we learn that Albany's and Cornwall's armies are on the march toward the French camp at Dover. The play is rushing toward a conclusion, for all the characters' trajectories have begun to converge.

ACT IV, SCENES VI–VII

SUMMARY: ACT IV, SCENE VI

Still disguised, Edgar leads Gloucester toward Dover. Edgar pretends to take Gloucester to the cliff, telling him that they are going up steep ground and that they can hear the sea. Finally, he tells Gloucester that they are at the top of the cliff and that looking down from the great height gives him vertigo. He waits quietly nearby as Gloucester prays to the gods to forgive him. Gloucester can no longer bear his suffering and intends to commit suicide. He falls to the ground, fainting.

Edgar wakes Gloucester up. He no longer pretends to be Poor Tom but now acts like an ordinary gentleman, although he still doesn't tell Gloucester that he is his son. Edgar says that he saw him fall all the way from the cliffs of Dover and that it is a miracle that he is still alive. Clearly, Edgar states, the gods do not want Gloucester to die just yet. Edgar also informs Gloucester that he saw the creature who had been with him at the top of the cliff and that this creature was not a human being but a devil. Gloucester accepts Edgar's explanation that the gods have preserved him and resolves to endure his sufferings patiently.

Lear, wandering across the plain, stumbles upon Edgar and Gloucester. Crowned with wild flowers, he is clearly mad. He babbles to Edgar and Gloucester, speaking both irrationally and with a strange perceptiveness. He recognizes Gloucester, alluding to Gloucester's sin and source of shame—his adultery. Lear pardons Gloucester for this crime, but his thoughts then follow a chain of associations from adultery to copulation to womankind, culminating in a tirade against women and sexuality in general. Lear's disgust carries him to the point of incoherence, as he deserts iambic pentameter (the verse form in which his speeches are written) and spits out the words "Fie, fie, fie! pah! pah!" (IV.vi.126).

Cordelia's people enter seeking King Lear. Relieved to find him at last, they try to take him into custody to bring him to Cordelia. When Lear runs away, Cordelia's men follow him.

Oswald comes across Edgar and Gloucester on the plain. He does not recognize Edgar, but he plans to kill Gloucester and collect the reward from Regan. Edgar adopts yet another persona, imitating the dialect of a peasant from the west of England. He defends Gloucester and kills Oswald with a cudgel. As he dies, Oswald entrusts Edgar with his letters.

Gloucester is disappointed not to have been killed. Edgar reads with interest the letter that Oswald carries to Edmund. In the letter, Goneril urges Edmund to kill Albany if he gets the opportunity, so that Edmund and Goneril can be together. Edgar is outraged; he decides to keep the letter and show it to Albany when the time is right. Meanwhile, he buries Oswald nearby and leads Gloucester off to temporary safety.

SUMMARY: ACT IV, SCENE VII

In the French camp, Cordelia speaks with Kent. She knows his real identity, but he wishes it to remain a secret to everyone else. Lear, who has been sleeping, is brought in to Cordelia. He only partially recognizes her. He says that he knows now that he is senile and not in his right mind, and he assumes that Cordelia hates him and wants to kill him, just as her sisters do. Cordelia tells him that she forgives him for banishing her.

Meanwhile, the news of Cornwall's death is repeated in the camp, and we learn that Edmund is now leading Cornwall's troops. The battle between France and England rapidly approaches.

ANALYSIS: ACT IV, SCENES VI–VII

Besides moving the physical action of the play along, these scenes forward the play's psychological action. The strange, marvelous scene of Gloucester's supposed fall over the nonexistent cliffs of Dover, Lear's mad speeches to Gloucester and Edgar in the wilderness, and the redemptive reconciliation between Cordelia and her not-quite-sane father all set the stage for the resolution of the play's emotional movement in Act V.

The psychological motivations behind Gloucester's attempted suicide and Edgar's manipulation of it are complicated and ambiguous. Gloucester's death wish, which reflects his own despair at the cruel, uncaring universe—and perhaps the play's despair as well—would surely have been troubling to the self-consciously Christian society of Renaissance England. Shakespeare gets around much of the problem by setting *King Lear* in a pagan past; despite the fact that the play is full of Christian symbols and allusions, its characters pray only to the gods and never to the Christian God.

Clearly, Edgar wants his father to live. He refuses to share in Gloucester's despair and still seeks a just and happy resolution to the events of the play. In letting Gloucester think that he has attempted suicide, Edgar manipulates Gloucester's understanding of divine will: he says to Gloucester after the latter's supposed fall and rebirth, "Thy life's a miracle.... / ... / The clearest gods ... / ... have preserved thee" (IV.vi.55, 73–74). Edgar not only stops Gloucester's suicidal thoughts but also shocks him into a rebirth. He tells his father that he should "bear free and patient thoughts": his life has been given back to him and he should take better care of it from now on (IV.vi.80).

In these scenes, King Lear's madness brings forth some of his strangest and most interesting speeches. As Edgar notes, Lear's apparent ramblings are "matter and impertinency mixed! / Reason in madness!" (IV.vi.168–169). This description is similar to Polonius's muttering behind Hamlet's back in *Hamlet*: "Though this be madness, yet there is method in't" (*Hamlet*, II.ii.203–204). Some of Lear's rambling does indeed seem to be meaningless babble, as when he talks about mice, cheese, and giants. But Lear swiftly moves on to talk of more relevant things. He finally understands that his older daughters, in Act I, scene i, and before, were sweet-talking him: "They flattered me like a dog. . . . To say 'aye' and 'no' to everything that I said!" (IV.vi.95–98).

Lear has realized, despite what flatterers have told him and he has believed, that he is as vulnerable to the forces of nature as any human being. He cannot command the rain and thunder and is not immune to colds and fever (the "ague" of IV.vi.103). Just as, during the storm, he recognizes that beneath each man's clothing is "a poor, bare, forked animal" (III. iv. 99–100), Lear now understands that no amount of flattery and praise can make a king different from anyone else: "Through tattered clothes small vices do appear; / Robes and furred gowns hide all" (IV.vi.158–159).

Armed with this knowledge, Lear can finally reunite with Cordelia and express his newfound humility and beg repentance. "I am a very foolish fond old man" (IV.vii.61), he tells her sadly, and he admits that she has "some cause" to hate him (IV.vii.76). Cordelia's moving response ("No cause, no, cause") seals their reconciliation (IV.vii.77). Love and forgiveness, embodied in Lear's best daughter, join with humility and repentance, and, for a brief time, happiness prevails. But the forces that Lear's initial error unleashed—Goneril, Regan, and Edmund, with all their ambition and appetite for destruction—remain at large. We thus turn from happy reconciliation to conflict, as Cordelia leads her troops against the evil that her father's folly has set loose in Britain.

ACT V, SCENES I–II

SUMMARY: ACT V, SCENE I

In the British camp near Dover, Regan asks Edmund if he loves Goneril and if he has found his way into her bed. Edmund responds in the negative to both questions. Regan expresses jealousy of her sister and beseeches Edmund not to be familiar with her.

Abruptly, Goneril and Albany enter with their troops. Albany states that he has heard that the invading French army has been joined by Lear and unnamed others who may have legitimate grievances against the present government. Despite his sympathy toward Lear and these other dissidents, Albany declares that he intends to fight alongside Edmund, Regan, and Goneril to repel the foreign invasion. Goneril and Regan jealously spar over Edmund, neither willing to leave the other alone with him. The three exit together.

Just as Albany begins to leave, Edgar, now disguised as an ordinary peasant, catches up to him. He gives Albany the letter that he took from Oswald's body—the letter in which Goneril's involvement with Edmund is revealed and in which Goneril asks Edmund to kill Albany. Edgar tells Albany to read the letter and says that if Albany wins the upcoming battle, he can sound a trumpet and Edgar will provide a champion to defend the claims made in the letter. Edgar vanishes and Edmund returns. Edmund tells Albany that the battle is almost upon them, and Albany leaves. Alone, Edmund addresses the audience, stating that he has sworn his love to both Regan and Goneril. He debates what he should do, reflecting that choosing either one would anger the other. He decides to put off the decision until after the battle, observing that if Albany survives it, Goneril can take care of killing him herself. He asserts menacingly that if the British win the battle and he captures Lear and Cordelia, he will show them no mercy.

SUMMARY: ACT V, SCENE II
The battle begins. Edgar, in peasant's clothing, leads Gloucester to the shelter of a tree and goes into battle to fight on Lear's side. He soon returns, shouting that Lear's side has lost and that Lear and Cordelia have been captured. Gloucester states that he will stay where he is and wait to be captured or killed, but Edgar says that one's death occurs at a predestined time. Persuaded, Gloucester goes with Edgar.

ANALYSIS: ACT V, SCENES I–II
In these scenes, the battle is quickly commenced and just as quickly concluded. The actual fighting happens offstage, during the short Act V, scene ii. Meanwhile, the tangled web of affection, romance, manipulation, power, and betrayal among Goneril, Regan, Albany, and Edmund has finally taken on a clear shape. We learn from Edmund that he has promised himself to both sisters; we do not know whether he is lying to Regan when he states that he has not slept with Goneril. Nor can we deduce from Edmund's speech which of the sisters he prefers—or, in fact, whether he really loves either of them—but it is clear that he has created a problem for himself by professing love for both.

It is clear now which characters support Lear and Cordelia and which characters are against them. Albany plans to show Lear and Cordelia mercy; Edmund, like Goneril and Regan, does not. Since all of these characters are, theoretically, fighting on the same side—the British—it is unclear what the fate of the captured Lear and Cordelia will be.

Ultimately, the sense that one has in these scenes is of evil turning inward and devouring itself. As long as Lear and Gloucester served as victims, Goneril and Regan were united. Now, though, with power concentrated in their hands, they fall to squabbling over Edmund's affections. Edmund himself has come into his own, taking command of an army and playing the two queens off against each other. It is suddenly clear that he, more than anyone else, will benefit from Lear's division of the kingdom. Gloucester's bastard may, indeed, shortly make himself king.

ACT V, SCENE III

SUMMARY

> *Howl, howl, howl, howl! O, you are men of stones ...*
> (See QUOTATIONS, p. 55)

Edmund leads in Lear and Cordelia as his prisoners. Cordelia expects to confront Regan and Goneril, but Lear vehemently refuses to do so. He describes a vividly imagined fantasy, in which he and Cordelia live alone together like birds in a cage, hearing about the outside world but observed by no one. Edmund sends them away, giving the captain who guards them a note with instructions as to what to do with them. He doesn't make the note's contents clear to the audience, but he speaks ominously. The captain agrees to follow Edmund's orders.

Albany enters accompanied by Goneril and Regan. He praises Edmund for his brave fighting on the British side and orders that he produce Lear and Cordelia. Edmund lies to Albany, claiming that he sent Lear and Cordelia far away because he feared that they would excite the sympathy of the British forces and create a mutiny. Albany rebukes him for putting himself above his place, but Regan breaks in to declare that she plans to make Edmund her husband. Goneril tells Regan that Edmund will not marry her, but Regan, who is unexpectedly beginning to feel sick, claims Edmund as her husband and lord.

Albany intervenes, arresting Edmund on a charge of treason. Albany challenges Edmund to defend himself against the charge in a trial by combat, and he sounds the trumpet to summon his champion. While Regan, who is growing ill, is helped to Albany's tent, Edgar appears in full armor to accuse Edmund of treason and face him in single combat. Edgar defeats Edmund, and Albany cries out to Edgar to leave Edmund alive for questioning. Goneril tries to help the wounded Edmund, but Albany brings out the treacherous letter to show that he knows of her conspiracy against him. Goneril rushes off in desperation.

Edgar takes off his helmet and reveals his identity. He reconciles with Albany and tells the company how he disguised himself as a mad beggar and led Gloucester through the countryside. He adds that he revealed himself to his father only as he was preparing to fight Edmund and that Gloucester, torn between joy and grief, died.

A gentleman rushes in carrying a bloody knife. He announces that Goneril has committed suicide. Moreover, she fatally poisoned Regan before she died. The two bodies are carried in and laid out.

Kent enters and asks where Lear is. Albany recalls with horror that Lear and Cordelia are still imprisoned and demands from Edmund their whereabouts. Edmund repents his crimes and determines to do good before his death. He tells the others that he had ordered that Cordelia be hanged and sends a messenger to try to intervene.

Lear enters, carrying the dead Cordelia in his arms: the messenger arrived too late. Slipping in and out of sanity, Lear grieves over Cordelia's body. Kent speaks to Lear, but Lear barely recognizes him. A messenger enters and reveals that Edmund has also died. Lear asks Edgar to loosen Cordelia's button; then, just as Lear thinks that he sees her beginning to breathe again, he dies.

Albany gives Edgar and Kent their power and titles back, inviting them to rule with him. Kent, feeling himself near death, refuses, but Edgar seems to accept. The few remaining survivors exit sadly as a funeral march plays.

ANALYSIS

This long scene brings the play to its resolution, ending it on a note of relentless depression and gloom. Almost all of the main characters wind up dead; only Albany, Edgar, and Kent walk off the stage at the end, and the aging, unhappy Kent predicts his imminent demise. Goneril, Regan, Cordelia, and Lear lie dead onstage, and Edmund and Gloucester have passed away offstage. Albany philosophizes about his merciless end when he says, "All friends shall taste / The wages of their virtue, and all foes / The cup of their deserving" (V.iii.301–303). One can argue that these words suggest that, in some sense, order and justice have triumphed over villainy and cruelty, and that the world is a just place after all.

But one can also argue that Albany's words ring hollow: most of the virtuous characters die along with the villains, making it difficult to interpret the scene as poetic justice. Indeed, death seems to be a defining motif for the play, embracing characters indiscriminately. We may feel that the disloyal Goneril and Regan, the treacherous Edmund, the odious Oswald, and the brutal Cornwall richly deserve their deaths. But, in the last scene, when the audience expects some kind of justice to be doled out, the good characters—Gloucester, Cordelia, Lear—die as well, and their bodies litter the stage alongside the corpses of the wicked.

This final, harrowing wave of death raises, yet again, a question that has burned throughout the play: is there any justice in the world? Albany's suggestion that the good and the evil both ultimately get what they deserve does not seem to hold true. Lear, howling over Cordelia's body, asks, "Why should a dog, a horse, a rat, have life, / And thou no breath at all?" (V.iii.305–306). This question can be answered only with the stark truth that death comes to all, regardless of each individual's virtue or youth. The world of *King Lear* is not a Christian cosmos: there is no messiah to give meaning to suffering and no promise of an afterlife. All that *King Lear* offers is despair.

The play's emotional extremes of hope and despair, joy and grief, love and hate, are brought to the fore as well in this final scene. Lear's address to Cordelia at the beginning of the scene is strangely joyful. He creates an intimate world that knows only love: "We two alone will sing like birds i' the cage. / When thou dost ask me blessing, I'll kneel down, / And ask of thee forgiveness" (V.iii.9–11). This blissful vision, however, is countered by the terrible despair that Lear evokes at Cordelia's death: "Thou'lt come no more, / Never, never, never, never, never." (V.iii.306–307). Yet, despite his grief, Lear expires in a flash of utterly misguided hope, thinking that Cordelia is coming back to life. In a sense, this final, false hope is the most depressing moment of all.

Similarly, Gloucester, as Edgar announces, dies partly of joy: "his flawed heart— / . . . / 'Twixt two extremes of passion, joy and grief, / Burst smilingly" (V.iii.195–198). Even Edmund, learning of Goneril's and Regan's deaths, says, "Yet Edmund was beloved. / The one the other poisoned for my sake, / And after slew herself" (V.iii.238–240). Even the cruel Edmund thinks of love in his last moments, a reminder of the warmth of which his bastard birth deprived him. But for him and the two sister queens, as for everyone else in *King Lear,* love seems to lead only to death. In perhaps the play's final cruelty, the audience is left with only a terrifying uncertainty: the good and the evil alike die, and joy and pain both lead to madness or death.

The corpses on the stage at the end of the play, of the young as well as the old, symbolize despair and death—just as the storm at the play's center symbolizes chaos and madness. For Lear, at least, death is a mercy. As Kent says, "The wonder is, he hath endured so long" in his grief and madness (V.iii.315). For the others, however, we are left wondering whether there is any justice, any system of punishment and reward in the "tough world" of this powerful but painful play (V.iii.313).

Important Quotations Explained

1. Unhappy that I am, I cannot heave
   My heart into my mouth. I love your majesty
   According to my bond; no more nor less.

Cordelia speaks these words when she address her father, King Lear, who has demanded that his daughters tell him how much they love him before he divides his kingdom among them (I.i.90–92). In contrast to the empty flattery of Goneril and Regan, Cordelia offers her father a truthful evaluation of her love for him: she loves him "according to my bond"; that is, she understands and accepts without question her duty to love him as a father and king. Although Cordelia loves Lear better than her sisters do, she is unable to "heave" her heart into her mouth, as her integrity prevents her from making a false declaration in order to gain his wealth. Lear's rage at what he perceives to be her lack of affection sets the tragedy in motion. Cordelia's refusal to flatter Lear, then, establishes her virtue and the authenticity of her love, while bringing about Lear's dreadful error of judgment.

2.   Thou, nature, art my goddess; to thy law
      My services are bound. Wherefore should I
      Stand in the plague of custom, and permit
      The curiosity of nations to deprive me,
      For that I am some twelve or fourteen moonshines
      Lag of a brother? Why bastard? wherefore base?
      . . .
      Legitimate Edgar, I must have your land.
      Our father's love is to the bastard Edmund
      As to the legitimate. Fine word—"legitimate"!
      Well, my legitimate, if this letter speed,
      And my invention thrive, Edmund the base
      Shall top the legitimate. I grow; I prosper.
      Now, gods, stand up for bastards!

Edmund delivers this soliloquy just before he tricks his father, Gloucester, into believing that Gloucester's legitimate son, Edgar, is plotting against him (I.ii.1–22). "I grow; I prosper," he says, and these words define his character throughout the play. Deprived by his bastard birth of the respect and rank that he believes to be rightfully his, Edmund sets about raising himself by his own efforts, forging personal prosperity through treachery and betrayals. The repeated use of the epithet "legitimate" in reference to Edgar reveals Edmund's obsession with his brother's enviable status as their father's rightful heir. With its attack on the "plague of custom," this quotation embodies Edmund's resentment of the social order of the world and his accompanying craving for respect and power. He invokes "nature" because only in the unregulated, anarchic scheme of the natural world can one of such low birth achieve his goals. He wants recognition more than anything else—perhaps, it is suggested later, because of the familial love that has been denied him—and he sets about getting that recognition by any means necessary.

3.   O, reason not the need! Our basest beggars
     Are in the poorest thing superfluous.
     Allow not nature more than nature needs,
     Man's life's as cheap as beast's . . .

     . . .
     You heavens, give me that patience, patience I need!
     . . .
     If it be you that stir these daughters' hearts
     Against their father, fool me not so much
     To bear it tamely; touch me with noble anger,
     And let not women's weapons, water-drops,
     Stain my man's cheeks! No, you unnatural hags,

     . . .
     No, I'll not weep.
     I have full cause of weeping, but this heart
     Shall break into a hundred thousand flaws,
     Or ere I'll weep. O fool, I shall go mad!

Lear delivers these lines after he has been driven to the end of his rope by the cruelties of Goneril and Regan (II.iv.259–281). He rages against them, explaining that their attempts to take away his knights and servants strike at his heart. "O, reason not the need!" he cries, explaining that humans would be no different from the animals if they did not need more than the fundamental necessities of life to be happy. Clearly, Lear needs knights and attendants not only because of the service that they provide him but because of what their presence represents: namely, his identity, both as a king and as a human being. Goneril and Regan, in stripping Lear of the trappings of power, are reducing him to the level of an animal. They are also driving him mad, as the close of this quotation indicates, since he is unable to bear the realization of his daughters' terrible betrayal. Despite his attempt to assert his authority, Lear finds himself powerless; all he can do is vent his rage.

QUOTATIONS

4.   As flies to wanton boys are we to the gods;
      They kill us for their sport.

Gloucester speaks these words as he wanders on the heath after
being blinded by Cornwall and Regan (IV.i.37–38). They reflect
the profound despair that grips him and drives him to desire his
own death. More important, they emphasize one of the play's chief
themes—namely, the question of whether there is justice in the universe. Gloucester's philosophical musing here offers an outlook of
stark despair: he suggests that there is no order—or at least no *good*
order—in the universe, and that man is incapable of imposing his
own moral ideas upon the harsh and inflexible laws of the world.
Instead of divine justice, there is only the "sport" of vicious, inscrutable gods, who reward cruelty and delight in suffering. In many
ways, the events of the play bear out Gloucester's understanding of
the world, as the good die along with the wicked, and no reason is
offered for the unbearable suffering that permeates the play.

QUOTATIONS

5.   Howl, howl, howl, howl! O, you are men of stones:
        Had I your tongues and eyes, I'd use them so
        That heaven's vault should crack. She's gone forever!
        I know when one is dead, and when one lives;
        She's dead as earth.

Lear utters these words as he emerges from prison carrying Cordelia's body in his arms (V.iii.256–260). His howl of despair returns us again to the theme of justice, as he suggests that "heaven's vault should crack" at his daughter's death—but it does not, and no answers are offered to explain Cordelia's unnecessary end. It is this final twist of the knife that makes *King Lear* such a powerful, unbearable play. We have seen Cordelia and Lear reunited in Act IV, and, at this point, all of the play's villains have been killed off, leaving the audience to anticipate a happy ending. Instead, we have a corpse and a howling, ready-for-death old man. Indeed, the tension between Lear as powerful figure and Lear as animalistic madman explodes to the surface in Lear's "Howl, howl, howl, howl," a spoken rather than sounded vocalization of his primal instinct.

QUOTATIONS

KEY FACTS

FULL TITLE
The Tragedy of King Lear

AUTHOR
William Shakespeare

TYPE OF WORK
Play

GENRE
Tragedy

LANGUAGE
English

TIME AND PLACE WRITTEN
England, 1604–1605

DATE OF FIRST PUBLICATION
First Folio edition, 1623

PUBLISHER
John Heminge and Henry Condell, two senior members of
Shakespeare's acting troupe

NARRATOR
Not applicable (drama)

CLIMAX
Gloucester's blinding in Act III, scene vii

PROTAGONIST
Lear, king of Britain

ANTAGONISTS
Lear's daughters Goneril and Regan; Edmund, the bastard son
of Gloucester

SETTING (TIME)
Eighth century B.C.

SETTING (PLACE)
Various locations in England

FORESHADOWING

Goneril and Regan's plotting in Act I foreshadows their later cruel treatment of Lear.

TONE

Serious and tragic; the occasional bursts of comedy are uniformly dark

THEMES

Justice, authority versus chaos, reconciliation, redemption

MOTIFS

Madness, betrayal, death

SYMBOLS

Weather plays an important symbolic role in the play, notably in Act III, when the tremendous thunderstorm over the heath symbolizes Lear's rage and mounting insanity; the actual blindness of Gloucester symbolizes the moral blindness that plagues both Lear and Gloucester himself in their dealings with their children; the "wheel" of fortune is another symbol by means of which Edmund, at the end of the play, conceives of his fall from power back into insignificance.

STUDY QUESTIONS

1. *What does the storm in Act III symbolize?*

The storm powerfully symbolizes the chaos in Lear's mind: the violent tumult in the natural world reflects Lear's inner turmoil. But the storm also provides an example of the power of nature, from which not even a king is safe. Even as he challenges the storm, Lear recognizes his own mortality and human frailty—perhaps for the first time. The storm may also be a reference to the idea of divine justice, since tempests and thunder have been viewed in both Christian and pagan traditions as a demonstration of divine anger or power. Thus, the storm seems both to point out the weakness of Lear's royal power in the face of nature's supremacy and to imply that the gods are angry at the state of human affairs. Such anger is likely directed not only at Lear's enemies for their ruthless and cruel ambition but also at Lear for his initial callous treatment of Cordelia.

2.   *What role do women play in* KING LEAR?

The female characters in *King Lear* are powerful figures who are often as aggressive as, and at times more ruthless than, their male counterparts. Cordelia, who is pure, unselfish, and unflinchingly loyal, is a more standard Shakespearean woman than her strong, assertive, conspiratorial, violent, and regal sisters, Goneril and Regan. While the older sisters are clearly very different in personality from the youngest, and while Goneril and Regan are clearly villains, all three daughters resemble their father. In Goneril and Regan, the similarity rests in their pride, arrogance, and fierce temper; in Cordelia, it rests in her aura of royal dignity, courage, and uncompromising stubbornness. All three sisters help to propel the plot, and Goneril and Regan are even effective killers (Regan, most unusual for a Shakespearean woman, kills with a sword). The presence of these three women becomes even more interesting when we remember that, as often happens in Shakespeare, there are no mothers present in the play; Lear's and Gloucester's dead wives are mentioned neither by these men nor by their children. Without guidance from other females, the sisters actively pursue their desires as they themselves see fit.

STUDY QUESTIONS

3. *Analyze the relationship between madness and
    blindness in the play.*

The two elderly characters who suffer the most in the play are Lear
and Gloucester. Their stories are similar in many ways; however,
while Lear slowly goes mad, Gloucester is blinded but remains sane.
Shakespeare implies a parallel between the two conditions: Lear
and Gloucester both seem to be able to perceive certain things more
clearly after they lose their faculties. Lear realizes only as he begins to go mad that Cordelia loves him and that Goneril and Regan
are treacherous flatterers. He comes to understand the weakness
of human nature, the emptiness of royal claims to power, and the
similarity of all human beings as he rambles in his insanity. Similarly, Gloucester comes to understand which son is really good and
which is bad at the very moment of his blinding. Still, both Lear and
Gloucester sink into despair before their deaths. It is interesting to
note that Lear's eyesight fails in the moments just before he dies,
while Gloucester wishes himself insane, thinking he might thus bear
his misery more easily. This grim irony suggests a hopelessness that
contributes to the general gloom surrounding the play's end.

STUDY QUESTIONS

How to Write Literary Analysis

The Literary Essay: A Step-by-Step Guide

When you read for pleasure, your only goal is enjoyment. You might find yourself reading to get caught up in an exciting story, to learn about an interesting time or place, or just to pass time. Maybe you're looking for inspiration, guidance, or a reflection of your own life. There are as many different, valid ways of reading a book as there are books in the world.

When you read a work of literature in an English class, however, you're being asked to read in a special way: you're being asked to perform *literary analysis*. To analyze something means to break it down into smaller parts and then examine how those parts work, both individually and together. Literary analysis involves examining all the parts of a novel, play, short story, or poem—elements such as character, setting, tone, and imagery—and thinking about how the author uses those elements to create certain effects.

A literary essay isn't a book review: you're not being asked whether or not you liked a book or whether you'd recommend it to another reader. A literary essay also isn't like the kind of book report you wrote when you were younger, where your teacher wanted you to summarize the book's action. A high school- or college-level literary essay asks, "How does this piece of literature actually work?" "How does it do what it does?" and, "Why might the author have made the choices he or she did?"

The Seven Steps

No one is born knowing how to analyze literature; it's a skill you learn and a process you can master. As you gain more practice with this kind of thinking and writing, you'll be able to craft a method that works best for you. But until then, here are seven basic steps to writing a well-constructed literary essay:

  1. *Ask questions*
  2. *Collect evidence*
  3. *Construct a thesis*

LITERARY ANALYSIS

4. Develop and organize arguments
5. Write the introduction
6. Write the body paragraphs
7. Write the conclusion

---

1. ASK QUESTIONS

When you're assigned a literary essay in class, your teacher will often provide you with a list of writing prompts. Lucky you! Now all you have to do is choose one. Do yourself a favor and pick a topic that interests you. You'll have a much better (not to mention easier) time if you start off with something you enjoy thinking about. If you are asked to come up with a topic by yourself, though, you might start to feel a little panicked. Maybe you have too many ideas—or none at all. Don't worry. Take a deep breath and start by asking yourself these questions:

- **What struck you?** Did a particular image, line, or scene linger in your mind for a long time? If it fascinated you, chances are you can draw on it to write a fascinating essay.

- **What confused you?** Maybe you were surprised to see a character act in a certain way, or maybe you didn't understand why the book ended the way it did. Confusing moments in a work of literature are like a loose thread in a sweater: if you pull on it, you can unravel the entire thing. Ask yourself why the author chose to write about that character or scene the way he or she did and you might tap into some important insights about the work as a whole.

- **Did you notice any patterns?** Is there a phrase that the main character uses constantly or an image that repeats throughout the book? If you can figure out how that pattern weaves through the work and what the significance of that pattern is, you've almost got your entire essay mapped out.

- **Did you notice any contradictions or ironies?** Great works of literature are complex; great literary essays recognize and explain those complexities. Maybe the title (*Happy Days*) totally disagrees with the book's subject matter (hungry orphans dying in the woods). Maybe the main character acts one way around his family and a completely different way around his friends and associates. If you can find a way to explain a work's contradictory elements, you've got the seeds of a great essay.

KING LEAR ❧ 65

At this point, you don't need to know exactly what you're going to say about your topic; you just need a place to begin your exploration. You can help direct your reading and brainstorming by formulating your topic as a *question,* which you'll then try to answer in your essay. The best questions invite critical debates and discussions, not just a rehashing of the summary. Remember, you're looking for something you can *prove or argue* based on evidence you find in the text. Finally, remember to keep the scope of your question in mind: is this a topic you can adequately address within the word or page limit you've been given? Conversely, is this a topic big enough to fill the required length?

GOOD QUESTIONS

> *"Are Romeo and Juliet's parents responsible for the deaths of their children?"*
>
> *"Why do pigs keep showing up in* LORD OF THE FLIES*?"*
> *"Are Dr. Frankenstein and his monster alike? How?"*

BAD QUESTIONS

> *"What happens to Scout in* TO KILL A MOCKINGBIRD*?"*
> *"What do the other characters in* JULIUS CAESAR *think about Caesar?"*
>
> *"How does Hester Prynne in* THE SCARLET LETTER *remind me of my sister?"*

---

2. COLLECT EVIDENCE

Once you know what question you want to answer, it's time to scour the book for things that will help you answer the question. Don't worry if you don't know what you want to say yet—right now you're just collecting ideas and material and letting it all percolate. Keep track of passages, symbols, images, or scenes that deal with your topic. Eventually, you'll start making connections between these examples and your thesis will emerge.

Here's a brief summary of the various parts that compose each and every work of literature. These are the elements that you will analyze in your essay, and which you will offer as evidence to support your arguments. For more on the parts of literary works, see the Glossary of Literary Terms at the end of this section.

LITERARY ANALYSIS

ELEMENTS OF STORY   These are the *what*s of the work—what happens, where it happens, and to whom it happens.

- **Plot:** All of the events and actions of the work.

- **Character:** The people who act and are acted upon in a literary work. The main character of a work is known as the *protagonist*.

- **Conflict:** The central tension in the work. In most cases, the protagonist wants something, while opposing forces (antagonists) hinder the protagonist's progress.

- **Setting:** When and where the work takes place. Elements of setting include location, time period, time of day, weather, social atmosphere, and economic conditions.

- **Narrator:** The person telling the story. The narrator may straightforwardly report what happens, convey the subjective opinions and perceptions of one or more characters, or provide commentary and opinion in his or her own voice.

- **Themes:** The main idea or message of the work—usually an abstract idea about people, society, or life in general. A work may have many themes, which may be in tension with one another.

ELEMENTS OF STYLE   These are the *how*s—how the characters speak, how the story is constructed, and how language is used throughout the work.

- **Structure and organization:** How the parts of the work are assembled. Some novels are narrated in a linear, chronological fashion, while others skip around in time. Some plays follow a traditional three- or five-act structure, while others are a series of loosely connected scenes. Some authors deliberately leave gaps in their works, leaving readers to puzzle out the missing information. A work's structure and organization can tell you a lot about the kind of message it wants to convey.

- **Point of view:** The perspective from which a story is told. In *first-person point of view*, the narrator involves him or herself in the story. ("I went to the store"; "We watched in horror as the bird slammed into the window.") A first-person narrator is usually the protagonist of the work, but not always. In *third-person point of view*, the narrator does not participate in the story. A third-person narrator may closely follow a specific character, recounting that individual character's thoughts or experiences, or it may be what we call an *omniscient* narrator. Omniscient narrators see and know all: they can witness any event in any time or place and are privy to the inner thoughts and feelings of all characters. Remember that the narrator and the author are not the same thing!

- **Diction:** Word choice. Whether a character uses dry, clinical language or flowery prose with lots of exclamation points can tell you a lot about his or her attitude and personality.

- **Syntax:** Word order and sentence construction. Syntax is a crucial part of establishing an author's narrative voice. Ernest Hemingway, for example, is known for writing in very short, straightforward sentences, while James Joyce characteristically wrote in long, incredibly complicated lines.

- **Tone:** The mood or feeling of the text. Diction and syntax often contribute to the tone of a work. A novel written in short, clipped sentences that use small, simple words might feel brusque, cold, or matter-of-fact.

- **Imagery:** Language that appeals to the senses, representing things that can be seen, smelled, heard, tasted, or touched.

- **Figurative language:** Language that is not meant to be interpreted literally. The most common types of figurative language are *metaphors* and *similes*, which compare two unlike things in order to suggest a similarity between them— for example, "All the world's a stage," or "The moon is like a ball of green cheese." (Metaphors say one thing *is* another thing; similes claim that one thing is *like* another thing.)

3. CONSTRUCT A THESIS

When you've examined all the evidence you've collected and know how you want to answer the question, it's time to write your thesis statement. A *thesis* is a claim about a work of literature that needs to be supported by evidence and arguments. The thesis statement is the heart of the literary essay, and the bulk of your paper will be spent trying to prove this claim. A good thesis will be:

- **Arguable.** "*The Great Gatsby* describes New York society in the 1920s" isn't a thesis—it's a fact.

- **Provable through textual evidence**. "*Hamlet* is a confusing but ultimately very well-written play" is a weak thesis because it offers the writer's personal opinion about the book. Yes, it's arguable, but it's not a claim that can be proved or supported with examples taken from the play itself.

- **Surprising**. "Both George and Lenny change a great deal in *Of Mice and Men*" is a weak thesis because it's obvious. A really strong thesis will argue for a reading of the text that is not immediately apparent.

- **Specific**. "Dr. Frankenstein's monster tells us a lot about the human condition" is *almost* a really great thesis statement, but it's still too vague. What does the writer mean by "a lot"? *How* does the monster tell us so much about the human condition?

GOOD THESIS STATEMENTS

Question: In *Romeo and Juliet*, which is more powerful in shaping the lovers' story: fate or foolishness?

Thesis: "Though Shakespeare defines Romeo and Juliet as 'star-crossed lovers' and images of stars and planets appear throughout the play, a closer examination of that celestial imagery reveals that the stars are merely witnesses to the characters' foolish activities and not the causes themselves."

Question: How does the bell jar function as a symbol in Sylvia Plath's *The Bell Jar*?

Thesis: "A bell jar is a bell-shaped glass that has three basic uses: to hold a specimen for observation, to contain gases, and to maintain a vacuum. The bell jar appears in each of these capacities in *The Bell Jar*, Plath's semi-autobiographical novel, and each appearance marks a different stage in Esther's mental breakdown."

Question: Would Piggy in *The Lord of the Flies* make a good island leader if he were given the chance?

Thesis: "Though the intelligent, rational, and innovative Piggy has the mental characteristics of a good leader, he ultimately lacks the social skills necessary to be an effective one. Golding emphasizes this point by giving Piggy a foil in the charismatic Jack, whose magnetic personality allows him to capture and wield power effectively, if not always wisely."

4. DEVELOP AND ORGANIZE ARGUMENTS

The reasons and examples that support your thesis will form the middle paragraphs of your essay. Since you can't really write your thesis statement until you know how you'll structure your argument, you'll probably end up working on steps 3 and 4 at the same time.

There's no single method of argumentation that will work in every context. One essay prompt might ask you to compare and contrast two characters, while another asks you to trace an image through a given work of literature. These questions require different kinds of answers and therefore different kinds of arguments. Below, we'll discuss three common kinds of essay prompts and some strategies for constructing a solid, well-argued case.

TYPES OF LITERARY ESSAYS

- **Compare and contrast**

  Compare and contrast the characters of Huck and Jim in THE ADVENTURES OF HUCKLEBERRY FINN.

  Chances are you've written this kind of essay before. In an academic literary context, you'll organize your arguments the same way you would in any other class. You can either go *subject by subject* or *point by point*. In the former, you'll discuss one character first and then the second. In the latter, you'll choose several traits (attitude toward life, social status, images and metaphors associated with the character) and devote a paragraph to each. You may want to use a mix of these two approaches—for example, you may want to spend a paragraph a piece broadly sketching Huck's and Jim's personalities before transitioning into a paragraph or two that describes a few key points of comparison. This can be a highly effective strategy if you want to make a counterintuitive argument—that, despite seeming to be totally different, the two objects being compared are actually similar in a very important way (or vice versa). Remember that your essay should reveal something fresh or unexpected about the text, so think beyond the obvious parallels and differences.

- **Trace**

  Choose an image—for example, birds, knives, or eyes—and trace that image throughout MACBETH.

  Sounds pretty easy, right? All you need to do is read the play, underline every appearance of a knife in *Macbeth*, and then list them in your essay in the order they appear, right? Well, not exactly. Your teacher doesn't want a simple catalog of examples. He or she wants to see you make *connections* between those examples—that's the difference between summarizing and analyzing. In the *Macbeth* example above, think about the different contexts in which knives appear in the play and to what effect. In *Macbeth*, there are real knives and imagined knives; knives that kill and knives that simply threaten. Categorize and classify your examples to give them some order. Finally, always keep the overall effect in mind. After you choose and analyze your examples, you should come to some greater understanding about the work, as well as your chosen image, symbol, or phrase's role in developing the major themes and stylistic strategies of that work.

- **Debate**

   Is the society depicted in 1984 good for its citizens?

In this kind of essay, you're being asked to debate a moral, ethical, or aesthetic issue regarding the work. You might be asked to judge a character or group of characters (*Is Caesar responsible for his own demise?*) or the work itself (*Is* JANE EYRE *a feminist novel?*). For this kind of essay, there are two important points to keep in mind. First, don't simply base your arguments on your personal feelings and reactions. Every literary essay expects you to read and analyze the work, so search for evidence in the text. What do characters in *1984* have to say about the government of Oceania? What images does Orwell use that might give you a hint about his attitude toward the government? As in any debate, you also need to make sure that you define all the necessary terms before you begin to argue your case. What does it mean to be a "good" society? What makes a novel "feminist"? You should define your terms right up front, in the first paragraph after your introduction.

Second, remember that strong literary essays make contrary and surprising arguments. Try to think outside the box. In the *1984* example above, it seems like the obvious answer would be no, the totalitarian society depicted in Orwell's novel is *not* good for its citizens. But can you think of any arguments for the opposite side? Even if your final assertion is that the novel depicts a cruel, repressive, and therefore harmful society, acknowledging and responding to the counterargument will strengthen your overall case.

LITERARY ANALYSIS

5. WRITE THE INTRODUCTION

Your introduction sets up the entire essay. It's where you present your topic and articulate the particular issues and questions you'll be addressing. It's also where you, as the writer, introduce yourself to your readers. A persuasive literary essay immediately establishes its writer as a knowledgeable, authoritative figure.

An introduction can vary in length depending on the over-all length of the essay, but in a traditional five-paragraph essay it should be no longer than one paragraph. However long it is, your introduction needs to:

- **Provide any necessary context.** Your introduction should situate the reader and let him or her know what to expect. What book are you discussing? Which characters? What topic will you be addressing?

- **Answer the "So what?" question.** Why is this topic important, and why is your particular position on the topic noteworthy? Ideally, your introduction should pique the reader's interest by suggesting how your argument is surprising or otherwise counterintuitive. Literary essays make unexpected connections and reveal less-than-obvious truths.

- **Present your thesis.** This usually happens at or very near the end of your introduction.

- **Indicate the shape of the essay to come.** Your reader should finish reading your introduction with a good sense of the scope of your essay as well as the path you'll take toward proving your thesis. You don't need to spell out every step, but you do need to suggest the organizational pattern you'll be using.

Your introduction should not:

- **Be vague.** Beware of the two killer words in literary analysis: *interesting* and *important*. Of course the work, question, or example is interesting and important—that's why you're writing about it!

- **Open with any grandiose assertions.** Many student readers think that beginning their essays with a flamboyant statement such as, "Since the dawn of time, writers have been fascinated with the topic of free will," makes them sound important and commanding. You know what? It actually sounds pretty amateurish.

- **Wildly praise the work.** Another typical mistake student writers make is extolling the work or author. Your teacher doesn't need to be told that "Shakespeare is perhaps the greatest writer in the English language." You can mention a work's reputation in passing—by referring to *The Adventures of Huckleberry Finn* as "Mark Twain's enduring classic," for example—but don't make a point of bringing it up unless that reputation is key to your argument.

- **Go off-topic.** Keep your introduction streamlined and to the point. Don't feel the need to throw in all kinds of bells and whistles in order to impress your reader—just get to the point as quickly as you can, without skimping on any of the required steps.

---

6. WRITE THE BODY PARAGRAPHS

Once you've written your introduction, you'll take the arguments you developed in step 4 and turn them into your body paragraphs. The organization of this middle section of your essay will largely be determined by the argumentative strategy you use, but no matter how you arrange your thoughts, your body paragraphs need to do the following:

- **Begin with a strong topic sentence.** Topic sentences are like signs on a highway: they tell the reader where they are and where they're going. A good topic sentence not only alerts readers to what issue will be discussed in the following paragraph but also gives them a sense of what argument will be made *about* that issue. "Rumor and gossip play an important role in *The Crucible*" isn't a strong topic sentence because it doesn't tell us very much. "The community's constant gossiping creates an environment that allows false accusations to flourish" is a much stronger topic sentence— it not only tells us *what* the paragraph will discuss (gossip) but *how* the paragraph will discuss the topic (by showing how gossip creates a set of conditions that leads to the play's climactic action).

- **Fully and completely develop a single thought.** Don't skip around in your paragraph or try to stuff in too much material. Body paragraphs are like bricks: each individual

LITERARY ANALYSIS

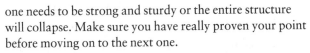

one needs to be strong and sturdy or the entire structure will collapse. Make sure you have really proven your point before moving on to the next one.

- **Use transitions effectively.** Good literary essay writers know that each paragraph must be clearly and strongly linked to the material around it. Think of each paragraph as a response to the one that precedes it. Use transition words and phrases such as *however, similarly, on the contrary, therefore,* and *furthermore* to indicate what kind of response you're making.

---

7. WRITE THE CONCLUSION

Just as you used the introduction to ground your readers in the topic before providing your thesis, you'll use the conclusion to quickly summarize the specifics learned thus far and then hint at the broader implications of your topic. A good conclusion will:

- **Do more than simply restate the thesis.** If your thesis argued that *The Catcher in the Rye* can be read as a Christian allegory, don't simply end your essay by saying, "And that is why *The Catcher in the Rye* can be read as a Christian allegory." If you've constructed your arguments well, this kind of statement will just be redundant.

- **Synthesize the arguments, not summarize them.** Similarly, don't repeat the details of your body paragraphs in your conclusion. The reader has already read your essay, and chances are it's not so long that they've forgotten all your points by now.

- **Revisit the "So what?" question.** In your introduction, you made a case for why your topic and position are important. You should close your essay with the same sort of gesture. What do your readers know now that they didn't know before? How will that knowledge help them better appreciate or understand the work overall?

- **Move from the specific to the general.** Your essay has most likely treated a very specific element of the work—a single character, a small set of images, or a particular passage. In your conclusion, try to show how this narrow discussion has wider implications for the work overall. If your essay on *To Kill a Mockingbird* focused on the character of Boo Radley, for example, you might want to include a bit in your conclusion about how he fits into the novel's larger message about childhood, innocence, or family life.

- **Stay relevant.** Your conclusion should suggest new directions of thought, but it shouldn't be treated as an opportunity to pad your essay with all the extra, interesting ideas you came up with during your brainstorming sessions but couldn't fit into the essay proper. Don't attempt to stuff in unrelated queries or too many abstract thoughts.

- **Avoid making overblown closing statements.** A conclusion should open up your highly specific, focused discussion, but it should do so without drawing a sweeping lesson about life or human nature. Making such observations may be part of the point of reading, but it's almost always a mistake in essays, where these observations tend to sound overly dramatic or simply silly.

A+ Essay Checklist

Congratulations! If you've followed all the steps we've outlined above, you should have a solid literary essay to show for all your efforts. What if you've got your sights set on an A+? To write the kind of superlative essay that will be rewarded with a perfect grade, keep the following rubric in mind. These are the qualities that teachers expect to see in a truly A+ essay. How does yours stack up?

- ✓ Demonstrates a thorough understanding of the book
- ✓ Presents an original, compelling argument
- ✓ Thoughtfully analyzes the text's formal elements
- ✓ Uses appropriate and insightful examples
- ✓ Structures ideas in a logical and progressive order
- ✓ Demonstrates a mastery of sentence construction, transitions, grammar, spelling, and word choice

Suggested Essay Topics

1. *Is Lear a sympathetic character? What about Gloucester? How do our impressions of them change during the course of the play?*

2. *Analyze the function that the Fool serves. Why does he disappear from the action?*

3. *Discuss the relationship between Cordelia and Lear, and compare it to the relationship between Edgar and Gloucester.*

4. *Of the three villains—Edmund, Goneril, and Regan—who is the most interesting? Why?*

5. *Discuss the significance of old age and death in* KING LEAR.

6. *How does order break down in Britain during the course of the play? Who is to blame?*

7. *Discuss Edmund. Are we meant to find him sympathetic?*

A+ Student Essay

> Examine the animal imagery that Shakespeare uses
> throughout *King Lear*. What purpose do these images
> serve? How do they relate to major themes in the play?

In *King Lear*, Shakespeare uses animal imagery to suggest that men
have very little power over their own fates and to emphasize the vul-
nerability of some of his most regal-seeming characters. He further
reinforces the idea of man's helplessness through his recurring allusions to the gods, which imply that the gods don't really care about
helping or protecting people on earth. Shakespeare also emphasizes
human frailty by repeatedly suggesting that man is "nothing," a
speck of dust that could blow away at any instant. The animal
images therefore introduce a frightening, recurring theme of weakness: even a king can die as suddenly and pointlessly as an ant.

Shakespeare's references to animals show that people are not
as unique and powerful as they seem. Stripped of his fancy clothing, Edgar is just "a worm" to his father; only a few alterations to
his status and appearance reveal him to be a weak, fragile creature
endangered by a storm. Lear likens people to animals when he
excuses Gloucester for the apparent sin of adultery, arguing that
human beings are no better than the lusty wren and "the small
gilded fly." Mourning Cordelia's death, Lear wonders why a rat
or dog should have life while his own young, extraordinarily wise
daughter should be murdered without warning. Each of these animal images suggests that humans do not enjoy special status on
earth, for they fall prey to the same sudden twists of fate and the
same base appetites that dominate the animal world.

Likewise, Shakespeare's discussion of the gods suggests that people are extremely vulnerable, for he describes an alternately sadistic
and uninterested set of divine "protectors" who are supposed to
be watching over the human race. When Gloucester worries that
storms are a sign of the gods' disfavor, Edmund posits the much
more frightening notion that there are no gods at all, and a trust in
divine intervention is "the excellent foppery of the world." Gloucester later makes the memorable observation that man is to god as
fly is to man, again discouraging anyone who would believe in the
presence of loving, compassionate deities who guide and protect
mankind. Noting the absence of cosmic justice in the world, Albany

LITERARY ANALYSIS

concludes that "humanity must perforce prey on itself, like monsters of the deep." Again and again, the gods are described as either cruel or nonexistent, leaving humans to behave as weak, predatory, and immoral animals.

Shakespeare drives home his ideas about man's animal nature by repeatedly describing his characters as "nothing," mere breaths of life that could expire at any moment. Without honorifics and luxuries, Lear observes, man's life is nothing, "as cheap as a beast's." Homeless, stripped naked in a storm, Lear asks, "Is man no more than this?" and concludes that humans are nothing more than "poor, bare, fork'd animals." In a split second, Edgar loses his title and family standing and observes, "Edgar I nothing am." The Fool reinforces Lear's sense of weakness by calling him "nothing" and suggesting that Lear was wrong to relinquish the few claims to power and wealth that made him unique. Repeatedly, Shakespeare likens his characters to "nothing," implying that human life is extremely fragile and possibly no more valuable than the life of a fly or beast.

By including so many images of animals, from lustful wrens to filthy worms, Shakespeare calls into question the idea that humans have any sort of special status or invincibility on earth. His characters frequently doubt the motives of the gods, reinforcing the sense that humans lack unique protection from the cosmos as they stumble blindly through life. Over and over, Shakespeare likens man to "nothing" and implies that a single life is much cheaper and more fragile than its possessor would like to believe. In *King Lear,* men are no better than dogs and rats, prone to the same undignified behavior, powerless before the same constant and inexplicable twists of fate.

GLOSSARY OF LITERARY TERMS

ANTAGONIST

The entity that acts to frustrate the goals of the *protagonist*. The antagonist is usually another *character* but may also be a non-human force.

ANTIHERO / ANTIHEROINE

A *protagonist* who is not admirable or who challenges notions of what should be considered admirable.

CHARACTER

A person, animal, or any other thing with a personality that appears in a *narrative*.

CLIMAX

The moment of greatest intensity in a text or the major turning point in the *plot*.

CONFLICT

The central struggle that moves the *plot* forward. The conflict can be the *protagonist*'s struggle against fate, nature, society, or another person.

FIRST-PERSON POINT OF VIEW

A literary style in which the *narrator* tells the story from his or her own *point of view* and refers to himself or herself as "I." The narrator may be an active participant in the story or just an observer.

HERO / HEROINE

The principal *character* in a literary work or *narrative*.

IMAGERY

Language that brings to mind sense-impressions, representing things that can be seen, smelled, heard, tasted, or touched.

MOTIF

A recurring idea, structure, contrast, or device that develops or informs the major *themes* of a work of literature.

NARRATIVE

A story.

LITERARY ANALYSIS

NARRATOR

The person (sometimes a *character*) who tells a story; the *voice* assumed by the writer. The narrator and the author of the work of literature are not the same person.

PLOT

The arrangement of the events in a story, including the sequence in which they are told, the relative emphasis they are given, and the causal connections between events.

POINT OF VIEW

The *perspective* that a *narrative* takes toward the events it describes.

PROTAGONIST

The main *character* around whom the story revolves.

SETTING

The location of a *narrative* in time and space. Setting creates mood or atmosphere.

SUBPLOT

A secondary *plot* that is of less importance to the overall story but may serve as a point of contrast or comparison to the main plot.

SYMBOL

An object, *character*, figure, or color that is used to represent an abstract idea or concept. Unlike an *emblem*, a symbol may have different meanings in different contexts.

SYNTAX

The way the words in a piece of writing are put together to form lines, phrases, or clauses; the basic structure of a piece of writing.

THEME

A fundamental and universal idea explored in a literary work.

TONE

The author's attitude toward the subject or *characters* of a story or poem or toward the reader.

VOICE

An author's individual way of using language to reflect his or her own personality and attitudes. An author communicates voice through *tone, diction*, and *syntax*.

LITERARY ANALYSIS

A NOTE ON PLAGIARISM

Plagiarism—presenting someone else's work as your own—rears its ugly head in many forms. Many students know that copying text without citing it is unacceptable. But some don't realize that even if you're not quoting directly, but instead are paraphrasing or summarizing, *it is plagiarism* unless you cite the source.

Here are the most common forms of plagiarism:

- Using an author's phrases, sentences, or paragraphs without citing the source
- Paraphrasing an author's ideas without citing the source
- Passing off another student's work as your own

How do you steer clear of plagiarism? You should *always* acknowledge all words and ideas that aren't your own by using quotation marks around verbatim text or citations like footnotes and endnotes to note another writer's ideas. For more information on how to give credit when credit is due, ask your teacher for guidance or visit www.sparknotes.com.

Review & Resources

Quiz

1. Lear is king of what country?

   A. France
   B. Britain
   C. East Anglia
   D. Scotland

2. Which one of Lear's daughters is sent into exile?

   A. Goneril
   B. Regan
   C. Cordelia
   D. Juliet

3. Which one of Lear's counselors reprimands the king for exiling his daughter?

   A. Albany
   B. Kent
   C. Cornwall
   D. Edmund

4. Who is Gloucester's bastard son?

   A. Kent
   B. Edgar
   C. Albany
   D. Edmund

5. When Lear visits Goneril, what does she demand of him?

   A. That he acknowledge her as the sole queen of the realm
   B. That he send away some of his knights
   C. That he execute Cordelia
   D. That he send away the Fool

6.   When they hear that Lear is coming to visit them, where do Regan and Cornwall go?

   A.   To Gloucester's castle
   B.   To France
   C.   To Goneril's home
   D.   To London

7.   Why is Kent thrown into the stocks?

   A.   For trying to kill Goneril
   B.   For beating Oswald with the flat of his sword
   C.   For threatening Lear's life
   D.   For praising Cordelia in public

8.   When he flees from his father, how does Edgar disguise himself?

   A.   As a common beggar
   B.   As a soldier
   C.   As Edmund
   D.   As Shakespeare

9.   When Lear tells Regan that Goneril has wronged him, what does Regan advise him to do?

   A.   Kill himself
   B.   Banish Goneril
   C.   Make Regan the sole queen
   D.   Go to Goneril and ask her forgiveness

10.   After he curses both Goneril and Regan, what does Lear do?

   A.   He storms out of Gloucester's castle, accompanied by the Fool
   B.   He disinherits both daughters
   C.   He sets out in search of Cordelia
   D.   He dies

11. Whom does Lear meet living in a little hovel on the heath?

    A.   Albany
    B.   Edgar, in disguise
    C.   Cordelia
    D.   Edmund

12. Why is Gloucester accused of treason?

    A.   Because he attempts to assassinate Goneril and Regan
    B.   Because he throws Lear in prison
    C.   Because he exiles Edgar
    D.   Because Edmund reveals letters showing that he knows of a French invasion

13. Where does Gloucester send Lear and his attendants?

    A.   To Dover
    B.   To London
    C.   To Gloucester's castle
    D.   To Goneril's castle

14. How is Gloucester punished for his "treason"?

    A.   He is burned
    B.   He is blinded
    C.   He is branded with a scarlet letter
    D.   He is exiled

15. Who encounters Gloucester on the heath and offers to lead him to Dover?

    A.   The Fool
    B.   Edmund
    C.   Edgar
    D.   Lear

16. Who is leading the army that lands at Dover?

    A.   Albany
    B.   Kent
    C.   Cordelia
    D.   Lear

17. Why does Gloucester want to reach the cliffs of Dover?

    A.   He wants to see the invasion fleet
    B.   He thinks Edgar is waiting for him there
    C.   He wants to throw himself over the cliffs
    D.   He wants to see the famed white cliffs before he dies

18. To whom are both Goneril and Regan attracted?

    A.   Edmund
    B.   Edgar
    C.   Albany
    D.   Cornwall

19. Before the battle between the French and English armies, to whose camp is Lear brought?

    A.   Cordelia's
    B.   Edmund's
    C.   Gloucester's
    D.   Albany's

20. What happens to Lear and Cordelia during the battle?

    A.   They are separated from one another
    B.   Edmund takes them captive
    C.   They are both killed
    D.   Cordelia is killed and Lear is taken captive

21. How does Regan die?

    A.   Edgar kills her
    B.   Edmund poisons her
    C.   She kills herself
    D.   Goneril poisons her

22. Who fights a duel with Edmund?

    A.   Albany
    B.   Gloucester
    C.   Edgar
    D.   Lear

23. What does Edmund reveal as he lies dying?

    A. That he ordered Cordelia killed

    B. That he is really Lear's son

    C. That he was in love with Cordelia

    D. That he killed Gloucester during the battle

24. What happens to Cordelia?

    A. She kills herself

    B. She is hanged in prison

    C. She marries Edgar

    D. She kills Goneril

25. What happens to Lear at the end of the play?

    A. His kingdom is restored

    B. He kills himself

    C. He orders Regan and Goneril executed

    D. He dies while weeping over Cordelia's body

REVIEW & RESOURCES

ANSWER KEY

1: B; 2: C; 3: B; 4: D; 5: B; 6: A; 7: B; 8: A; 9: D; 10: A; 11: B; 12: D;
13: A; 14: B; 15: C; 16: C; 17: C; 18: A; 19: A; 20: B; 21: D; 22: C;
23: A; 24: B; 25: D

Suggestions for Further Reading

BLOOM, HAROLD. *Shakespeare: The Invention of the Human.* New York: Riverhead Books/Penguin Putnam Inc., 1998.

DANSON, LAWRENCE, ed. *On* KING LEAR. Princeton: Princeton University Press, 1981.

EVANS, G. BLAKEMORE, et al., eds. *The Riverside Shakespeare.* Boston: Houghton Mifflin, 1974.

GREENBLATT, STEPHEN, gen. ed. *The Norton Shakespeare* (based on the Oxford edition). New York and London: W. W. Norton & Co., 1997.

IOPPOLO, GRACE. *William Shakespeare's* KING LEAR: *A Sourcebook.* New York: Routledge, 2003.

MACK, MAYNARD, JR. KING LEAR *in Our Time.* Berkeley: University of California Press, 1966.

ROSENBERG, MARVIN. *The Masks of* KING LEAR. Berkeley: University of California Press, 1972.

SHAKESPEARE, WILLIAM. KING LEAR. Ed. R.A. Foakes. Walton-on-Thames, Surrey, U.K.: Arden Shakespeare/Thomas Nelson and Sons, Ltd., 1997.

SMITH, EMMA. *The Cambridge Introduction to Shakespeare.* Cambridge: Cambridge University Press, 2007.